Nirala Series

Tamang Shamans

Dr. Larry Peters is a world renowned scholar and initiated shaman in the Tibetan tradition. He was the recipient of the Regent's Fellowship at the University of California and a post-doctoral fellow of the National Institute of Mental Health. Dr. Peters holds advance degrees in both Anthropology and Psychology. He has conducted ethnographic fieldwork in Nepal, China, Mongolia, and Siberia and is a research associate of the Foundation for Shamanic Studies. Dr. Peters has published extensively on shamanism and has conducted numerous experiential shamanic workshops in the United States, Europe, and Asia. Dr. Peters is a professor of Anthropology and Psychology at The California Graduate Institute of Professional Psychology and Psychoanalysis in Los Angeles, where he serves as Co-Director of both the Programs in Cross-Cultural Psychology and in Marriage Family and Child Counseling. Dr. Peters also teaches at Pacifica University in Santa Barbara. He is a Board Member of the Association of Transpersonal Psychology and a licensed psychotherapist in the State of California. For some of the clients in his private practice, Dr. Peters employs shamanic counseling methods to promote psycho-spiritual integration.

Tamang Shamans

An Ethnopsychiatric Study of Ecstasy and Healing in Nepal

LARRY PETERS

With an Introduction by
Jacques Maquet

Nirala

Nirala Publications
G.P.O. Box 7004
Daryaganj, New Delhi-110002
niralabooks@yahoo.co.in

First published in Nirala Series 1999
Paperback : 2007

ISBN-81-8250-009-5

Cover Design: Vimal Palival/Shakti

Printed at
H.S. Offset Printers
New Delhi-110002

Contents

Dedicated to my sacred Cow

List of Illustrations

1. The shaman, Bhirendra, dressed in pilgrimage attire, plays the drum and enters trance.

INTRODUCTION

Scholar and Shaman

A few months after Dr. Larry Peters had returned from the fieldwork on which this book is based, I paid a visit to his guru, the shaman Bhirendra, in Tin Chuli, the village where he lives. We talked about Larry's apprenticeship. During the conversation, I became aware that Bhirendra and I were speaking as two teachers who are addressing the progress of a doctoral candidate.

The image of the guru and the professor discussing the achievements and difficulties of their common disciple/student has remained with me. It perfectly epitomizes Larry Peters's endeavor to include the experience of a shaman's training within his scholarly research on Tamang shamanism.

Since then, Larry Peters has become a full-fledged colleague of his former Western teacher. He still has to complete the last stages of shamanistic training under his Eastern teacher. But he has been far enough up that road to gain the insider's perspective which makes this book a unique contribution to the psychology and anthropology of shamanism.

This book interprets the shaman's role in the Tamang segment of the Nepalese society as analogous to the psychotherapist's role in the contemporary Western world. This analogy has already been pointed out but it has rarely, if ever, been so convincingly demonstrated. In a detailed analysis of a few cases, Dr. Peters shows how Tamang shamans relieve the mental tensions of their patients, cure illnesses, and by doing so restore equilibrium in disturbed interpersonal relationships within a family or village community. It is sometimes by solving social conflicts that the shaman heals the afflicted. The shaman's training and the training of a Western psychotherapist offer some striking similarities: both are didactic (learning theories, procedures, and methods) and practical (the psychoanalyst's own training analysis, and the shaman apprentice's own mastered trance). The analogy extends to the treatments and procedures, and thereby accounts for the effectiveness of the shamanistic therapy.

For Dr. Peters, the shaman certainly remains a religious specialist but the socio- and psychotherapeutic dimensions of his role are given full recognition.

This book is important because it presents a thorough description of the hitherto little known Tamang shamanistic system, and because it proposes an interpretation of it which renews our understanding of shamanism in general. Also, methodologically, it is important because Peters skillfully explores the potentialities and limitations of the experiential approach. Let me point out some conclusions one may draw from Peters's practice of the experiential method in his Tamang research.

1

Peters did not become a Tamang, nor did he assume the social role of a shaman. He became an apprentice under a master shaman, and in the course of his training he agreed to be put in situations generating ecstatic states. This made it possible for him to observe in himself mental states similar to those experienced by the other disciples of the guru. By extension, this gave him inside understanding of shamanic trances in general. It made it possible for him to discuss these matters with informants who had gone through similar psychic processes.

In order to remain research-relevant, the stimulus-situation (for instance, softly drumming in a 3-3 pattern) and the inner response (for instance, automatically shaking) have to be well defined, as they are here. The stimulus-situation should not be extended to the totality of the behavioral patterns characteristic of a particular culture (such as "to live as Tamang do") and the response should not be accordingly generalized (such as "to feel as Tamang do"). This is why practicing the experiential approach does not mean or imply "going native."

Essential to the validity of the method is the assumption that foreign observers and local practitioners have a similar inner response to the same situation. There are good theoretical reasons to believe that this is so, such as the physiological uniformity of humankind, and the universality of the human condition. Yet the experiential similarity should be checked in each case. This is what Peters did. Bhirendra's discursive teachings, discussions with the master and other shamans, and external observations of ecstatic behaviors confirmed that the observer's inner experiences were analogous to what the others experienced.

2

A vigilant reader may object that, in fact, ecstatic experiences are, in one important respect, differently described by Peters and the Tamang. The latter consider them as possessions by ancestors or gods whereas Peters, after relating his involuntary shaking and "bouncing all over the room" during a trance, writes that he "felt no alien power enter" him.

The source of this discrepancy is to be found in the diverging world views held by Tamang and Peters. For the former, many spirits of different types inhabit the Tamang land and space, and constantly affect "the lives of men for good and evil." Spirits are present in the Tamang environment as much as germs and microbes in ours. When relating their experiences, Tamang project their intellectual conception of reality. They do the same when speaking of Peters's trances: they say he was possessed. Not surprisingly, Peters does not share the Tamang view that spirits are everywhere, and consequently he does not describe his experience in terms of possession.

I do not think that this divergence in culturally constructed realities affects the basic parallelism of experiences. As mentioned above, discussions of these experiences-as-recalled by those who have gone through them have established their essential similarity.

I would add that, unlike the Tamang, Peters is very careful in distinguishing the experience from its interpretation.

Nevertheless, not sharing a cultural world view certainly diminishes the degree of inner participation. And Peters, with an intellectual integrity to be commended, recognizes it. He says, "my personal circumstances, biases and lifestyle made it impossible to carry out a complete participatory inquiry."

3

The possibility of validly observing one's own mental processes –a necessary condition of the experiential approach–has often been questioned. The objection was that the observation of one's feelings, emotions, and thoughts interfered with them, and eventually made them disappear. Reports in this book demonstrate that mental processes, even as unusual as trances, may be observed. Peters was aware of his body movements during the trances, and this awareness did not make them disappear (what ended the trance was his fear that he was losing control).

Unobtrusive inner observation requires some training (as do other anthropological research procedures, such as interviewing without influencing the informant's answers). This training–not offered in graduate programs of anthropology–amounts to developing an attitude of mindfulness, an important part of the insight meditation practice. The meditator is instructed to notice affects and thoughts as soon as they arise in consciousness, and to observe them in a contemplative mental mode until they disappear. This mental mode excludes judging them, analyzing them, and identifying with them. Dr. Peters's previous meditation practice happens to have prepared him to observe the unfolding of inner phenomena without attempting to modify them.

The essential objective of the shamans' training is to make them able to control their trances. This is also achieved through awareness of what happens during the ecstatic states. Their patients, on the contrary, cannot master trances and, as Kanchi, do not remember what they said during the crisis.

4

The repeatability of obervations is the ultimate test of their scholarly value: statements that cannot be verified may be true, but they are outside the scope of the disciplines of knowledge. Would it be possible to replicate Peters's experiential study of Tamang shamanism in order to assess its reliability?

Yes, this would be possible to the same extent as any "conventional" anthropological field research can be repeated by other observers. First, it is possible because the psychic phenomena associated with Tamang shamanism are not idiosyncratic; they are traditional. Shamans, patients, and the village community expect them to occur over and over again in the same forms. The techniques which generate them are transmitted from guru to disciple, and masters preserve their continuity through the individual guidance of their trainees. Thus another anthropologist going after Peters to Boudha and Tin Chuli would find the same shamanic tradition in which the same type of ecstatic experiences are bound to be repeated.

Second, it is because Dr. Peters, following the scholarly tradition of openness, has not surrounded his research with secrecy. Any researcher who reads his research reports in this book and published articles is provided with the information necessary to duplicate Peters's original research. There is no mysterious and inaccessible shaman-informant (I met Bhirendra!).

Third, it is because Peters uses a precise and unambiguous terminology. 'Possession,' 'ecstasis,' 'enstasis,' and other crucial terms referring to observed phenomena are so defined as to permit comparison with data obtained by other researchers. Some emic categories, such as 'crazy visions' and 'clear visions,' meet the same criteria of comparability.

Finally, it is because Peters describes in detail the approach he used. Undergoing the training of a Tamang shaman apprentice in conditions similar to Peters's can be done by another anthropologist.

Patterned experiences, accessible field, precise conceptual tools, and fully described approach make it possible to repeat

Peters's research and to verify the reliability of his observations. Obviously it would not be the kind of repetition obtained under laboratory conditions. The usual circumstances of field research in social and cultural anthropology—observation, often informal, by an individual working alone in a small community for an extended period of time—limit the repeatability of observations. This is not the place to discuss the matter. The only point I wish to make here is that Dr. Larry Peters's inner observations can be repeated and verified no less—and no more—than the external observations of the more conventional field research.

In this book, his first, Larry Peters has extended the territory of psychological anthropology by his innovative and convincing use of the experiential approach. This is no ordinary achievement.

Jacques Maquet

CHAPTER ONE

Tamang Shamanism A Cross-Cultural Perspective

Shamanism is thought to be mankind's earliest religion, possibly dating back 100,000 years or more; it may well have been the religion of Neanderthal man (Furst 1972:viii-ix). Shamanism originated in association with the hunting-and-gathering way of life (LaBarre 1972a:162-163) and many researchers believe that the shaman's role is portrayed in the Upper Paleolithic cave art of southern France (Campbell 1959:299ff; Furst 1974; Lommel 1967:105ff). Moerman (1979:59) indicates that the first profession was that of shaman-curer.

The term shaman comes to us through Russian, from the Siberian Tungusic term *śaman*, meaning "one who is excited, moved, raised." This is descriptive of the most salient aspect of the shaman's trance: shaking (Casanowicz 1924:419). According to Professor Sir Harold Bailey, shaman ultimately derives from Vedic *sram* meaning "to heat oneself or practice austerities," and *śramaṇa* meaning monk or ascetic. This term made its way from India through central Asia to China (*sha-men*) and Japan (*shamon*) (Blacker 1975:317-318), entering Siberia via the dissemination of Tantric Buddhism (Mironov and Shirokogoroff 1924).

While the origin of the term is Asian, it is used by researchers to describe similar phenomena in many parts of the world (Eliade 1964; Peters and Price-Williams 1980), occurring not only among hunters but in contemporary peasant, nomadic and urban communities as well. In other words, shamanism appears to be a tenacious and adaptable profession (see Landy 1974).

The shaman is a specific type of religious specialist. Although defined differently from various perspectives, it is agreed that the shaman enters into a trance state on behalf of his/her community (Eliade 1964:23; Halifax 1979:21-22; Wallace 1966:150f). Thus shamanism describes a community-recognized religious vocation that involves the production of altered states of consciousness.[1] The function the shaman fulfills in the community is often equated with that of healer/psychotherapist (Levi-Strauss 1963: 193f; Torrey 1972). While important, healing is not the only defining characteristic of shamanism. Park (1938:10) suggests that "witchcraft may be as important a part of shamanism as the curing of disease or the charming of game." For example, among the Jivaro of South America, there are shamans who only perform bewitching functions, while other shamans are the curers (Harner 1973:19-23). In many cultures, the features of "black" and "white" shamans are combined in one person (Eliade 1964:299). Such is the case among the Tamang where the shaman uses his personal power (*śakti*)[2] any way he chooses. However, the Tamang shaman employs his powers primarily in trance-curing, only secondarily for witchcraft, and infrequently in securing the food supply.

In most cultures, the shaman, like other types of religious specialists, is concerned with the ultimate problems of life (birth,

[1] Krippner (1972:1) defines altered states of consciousness as "a mental state which can be subjectively recognized by an individual (or by an objective observer of the individual) as representing a *difference* in psychological functioning from the individual's "normal" alert waking state (see Ludwig 1969:9). More recently, Zinberg (1977:1) suggested using the term "alternate" rather than altered which has a pejorative connotation suggesting that such states represent deviation from the way consciousness ought to be. The word altered is employed here because it is in standard usage. However, I agree with Zinberg (1977:1) that "different states of consciousness prevail at different times for different reasons . . . *Alternate states of consciousness* is a plural, all-inclusive term, unlike *usual state of consciousness*, which is merely one specific state of ASC."

[2] The foreign terms in the text are in Nepali, unless otherwise indicated. The use of Nepali or Tamang is not arbitrary, but reflects spontaneous occurrence in interviews with shamans.

death, sickness, hunger) and their solutions. Shamans are distinguished from priests in that their authority rests on their personal experiences with the supernatural, whereas priests are liturgical officiants presiding at rituals and over congregations without the necessity of a personal direct experience with the deity (Lowie 1965:164; Park 1938:10; Wissler 1938:200f). Shamans may also be priests, however, and preside over congregations (see Myerhoff 1974:95) but their rituals contain experiential encounters with the supernatural.

For the most part, shamans are part-time specialists, and the income thus derived, if any, is only supplementary. Rank and privilege over his fellows is not necessarily contingent. Priests, on the other hand, are generally full-time specialists, and this vocation occurs predominantly in diversified and stratified societies (Malefijt 1968:235). In the acculturated situation in Nepal, such distinctions do not exist. Shamans and *lama* (priests) exist side by side, each representing different societal interests, both functioning on part-time bases.

In their descriptions of shamans, some scholars have emphasized intellectual qualities (Howells 1949:230; Murphy 1964:77; M. E. Opler 1936:1171f) and political influence (Berndt 1964: 268f; Halifax 1979:21; Murdock 1965:170-171). Maddox (1923: 25) described the shaman as the "great man of primitive times"; and, more recently, Landy (1974:103f) explored the shaman's innovative social role as "cultural broker" in situations of acculturation. Shweder (1972:412) pointed up the unique cognitive capacities of Zinacanteco shamans as opposed to non-shamans, especially their ability to "avoid bafflement and impose form on unstructured stimuli."

The Shaman's Trance

One of the most authoritative ethnographic studies of shamanism is Shirokogoroff's (1935) *Psychomental Complex of the Tungus*. He (*ibid*:268,271) described the shaman's most basic attribute as the "mastery of spirits." He observed that the shaman, in his trances, controls the spirits using his body as a "placing" into which spirits are induced and exorcised. In other words, a dominant feature of the shaman's trance is possession.[3] The Tungus distinguish between an individual who is involuntarily possessed (interpreted as illness) and the shaman who "possesses spirits." These two different types of trance that Shirokogoroff observed among the Tungus, i.e., that of the victim and that of the shaman, are also reported by researchers from various other culture areas. Oesterreich (1966:131ff) refers to them as "spontaneous" and "voluntary" respectively; Bourguignon (1968:6-7) calls them "negative" and "positive"; Lewis (1971:55) "unsolicited" and "solicited."

While some investigators emphasize possession as the primary aspect of shamanism (Shirokogoroff 1935:271; Loeb 1929:62-63), others contend that the true shaman experiences only visionary magical flight[4] (Eliade 1964; Heusch 1962). Lewis (1971:49) cautions against interpreting shamanism as exclusive to either phenomenon, and instead posits a definition that includes both magical flight and spirit possession, noting that they can exist separately or coexist in various degrees (also see Reinhard 1976). In a cross-cultural survey of 42 cultures in which shamanism is reported, Peters and Price-Williams (1980:418) found 18 reporting spirit possession only, 10 magical flight only, 11 both, and in 3 neither concept was used to explain the trance state. Again, the crucial element is control of trance. There seems to be no reason to restrict the concept of shamanism to any one of these limiting interpretations. Shamanism is obviously inclusive of a diverse set

[3] Crapanzano (1977:7) defines possession as "any altered state of consciousness indigenously interpreted in terms of the influence of an alien spirit."

[4] After Eliade (1964), the term "magical flight" is used to connote an altered state of consciousness interpreted as "soul journey" to heaven, other worlds, underground, or horizontally (to places in this world). An important variant of soul journey is the sending of a familiar or tutelary spirit on the journey. Both types are psychologically similar in that they involve the "seeing of visions."

of trance phenomena, all of which have the experiential feature of control.

Similarly, Firth (1959:129-148; 1964) applies the term shaman to describe those who enter into controlled trances and manipulate spirits in socially recognized ways ("master of spirits"), and in this way also distinguishes between shamans and spirit mediums. From a psychological perspective, however, the distinctions between shamans and mediums are somewhat unclear. The gods often possess and communicate through shamans, and mediums are said to have controlled trances. As Firth (1967a: 198-199) writes, " . . . control is important . . . for the mediumistic state must be able to be induced and not simply have to rely on spontaneous generation. Mediums must be able to go into trance when people are ill. . . . Every spirit medium has some form of internal control by which he is enabled to return from his state of dissociation to his ordinary condition." Given these conditions, it could be very difficult to distinguish a proficient medium from a shaman.

Lewis (1971:92f) argues that shamans and mediums are sometimes linked, representing stages in an ongoing initiatory process culminating in shamanism. The primary phase common to both is a spontaneous "initiatory possession" seen as illness. The second phase consists of becoming a medium; herein the possessions become volitional and practiced in community context. In the third phase, the medium becomes a full-fledged shaman if he gains mastery over the spirits that possess him; no longer a passive oracle of the gods, the shaman establishes a "master-to-servant" relationship over them (Shirokogoroff 1935:271).

What is important, from the psychological point of view, is not the belief in spirit mastery but mastery of the trance. There are religious specialists who attain full control of their trances and use them in socio-cultural context, but who do not associate their states with beliefs about spirits. For example, the Azande witchdoctor induces trances through "violent ecstatic" dance, reports visions, slashes his tongue and chest with knives, and extracts objects from the bodies of patients. But his powers are thought to emanate from a "magic inside of him." Illness, according to

Azande belief, does not derive from a spirit but from witchcraft and sorcery; i.e., from other people. Therefore, combatting illness does not demand manipulation of other-worldly beings (Evans-Pritchard 1976:73,87f). Likewise, the !Kung Bushman medicine man derives his power from inside of himself during trance states, not through the control and utilization of spirits (Lee 1968:50f).

It is crucial not to get lost in the quagmire of terms, or to be restricted to one specific cultural group and area, if the term shaman is to have a generic and cross-cultural application. Therefore, it does not seem significant how the trance is interpreted, or what the researcher calls the specialist (medicine man, witch-doctor, magician, shaman). What seems pertinent are the elements of control and volition of the trance state. These are the elements that recur in ethnographic descriptions of shamans and their trances. Peters and Price-Williams (1980:418) found this to be the case in 100% of the 42 cultures detailed in their study.

A wide variety of techniques are employed by shamans to induce trance, ranging from fasting and other deprivations to dancing and the use of percussion instruments (Needham 1967) like the drum which, when beaten at certain rapid rates, may facilitate trance states (Neher 1961, 1962; see Sturtevant 1968). There are also "meditative"-type trances like those employed by aboriginal shamans who sit or lie in "quiet contemplative states" when communicating with the supernatural and performing magical acts (Elkin 1977:56). Some of the earliest forms of shamanism, dating back to the Paleolithic, may have involved the ingestion of hallucinogenic substances (Wasson 1968; LaBarre 1972b:270f). The shamanistic use of drugs was common in Siberia (Jochelson 1908: 583), and in both Americas (see Furst 1976). Again, the common element of all these accounts is that the shaman, no matter how the trance is interpreted (magical flight, spirit possession, etc.), or how produced (drumming, dancing, etc.), remains in control of his trance. The shaman is not overwhelmed by the intensity of his experience but manipulates it in the service of his community.

Enstasis or *samādhi* (Skt.), the goal of certain types of Eastern meditations and yoga, has been distinguished from ecstasy by Fischer (1972) according to their respective levels of neurological arousal (hypoaroused vs. hyperaroused) and whether they are hallucinatory or not. Naranjo (1971:6ff,96-97) sees the shaman's trance as Dionysian and ecstatic and he distinguishes it from the concentrated self-absorption characteristic of the quieter forms of meditation.

Such categories, however, are not adequate to distinguish the shaman's trance from other types of trance. As mentioned earlier, the shaman's trance can be either hypoactive or hyperactive. In Nepal, the Tamang shaman may begin his trance with a frenzied dance that ends in a passive hypoaroused state from which he reports visions similar to those related by Australian shamans in their tranquil trance state. Elkin (1977:45f) mentions many similarities between the trances of aboriginal shamans and accounts of Indo-Tibetan mystics.

Like the yogi or meditator, the shaman experiences altered states of consciousness as part of a definite discipline. There is a guru-disciple relationship, a system of psychological techniques and prescribed types of altered states of consciousness whose goal is the psychological transformation of the individual (see Chapter 6). But the transformation being sought by the shaman is much different from the ideals of Hindu and Buddhist yoga philosophy. It belongs to a different historical period and ethos formed under very different cultural conditions.

The shaman is not a seeker of enlightenment nor does he seek detachment, as does the yogi. The shaman's trance is distinct from *samādhi* in that it does not have the same goal. In the *Yogasara-Saṅgraha* of Vijñānabiksu, *samādhi* is defined as an invulnerable state in which perception of the external world is absent (see Eliade 1958a:78-80). The shaman's trance, on the other hand, is outwardly oriented. It is not autonomous but directed toward the community so that the trance serves as a medium of communication between the supernatural or non-ordinary reality and the community of men. Peters and Price-Williams (1980:418) found that the entranced shaman remained in communicative rapport with audience and patient in 81% of the 42 cultures surveyed. For example, Harner (1973:23-25) reports that the Jivaro shaman has visions under the influence of narcotics, and sucks pathogenic "objects" from his patient's body saying "Now I have sucked it out. Here it is." The Tungus shaman goes on magical flight to upper and lower worlds, yet still answers questions put to him by spectators and reports his perilous visionary journey (Shirokogoroff 1935:340ff, 363). Further, the interaction between audience and shaman is so important to the Tungus shamans that they believe ecstasy will end if the audience ceases singing and encouraging. This relationship is described as one of mutual excitement: shaman and audience influence the trance of the other.

These two factors, control and communicative rapport, along with memory (see Chapter 6), are the most significant psychological elements of the Tamang shaman's trance. While the Tamang shamans do not take hallucinogens, they do manifest all the aspects of shamanism discussed above. They become possessed voluntarily and embark on magical flights on which they have visions of deities and non-ordinary worlds that are utilized in the service of their patients and community.

Psychopathology and Shamanism

Tamang shamans are "called" to their profession through a crisis-type experience typical of many Asian shamans. As opposed to a deliberate "vision quest" as occurs in North America, for example, the Tamang shaman is "inflicted" by the spirits (see Bogoras 1930:442-443). During his crisis, a Tamang shaman is beset with anxiety, hallucinations, convulsions, and the desire for solitude. All these symptoms are indigenously interpreted as abnormal; that is, involuntary spirit possession or soul loss. One becomes a shaman by overcoming these crises and mastering the symptoms.

Investigators have ascribed various psychological interpretations to the shaman's calling, ranging from depressive psychosis that can lead to suicide (Lot-Falck 1970) to acute schizophrenia (Silverman 1967). Even the final outcome (i.e., passage through the neophyte stage) has been likened to a "controlled hysterical dissociation" supported by the culture, thereby saving the individual from a "wildly disturbed schizophrenic state" (Wallace 1966:150f). Devereux (1956:28-29; 1961:63-64) says, "the shaman is mentally deranged," adding that shamanism is a neurotic defense which never attains sublimation so that, sooner or later, the shaman will decompensate into a pathological condition. Conversely, some writers emphasize the therapeutic aspects of the shaman's initiatory process. Ackerknecht (1943:46) states that "shamanism is not a disease but being healed from a disease. . . ." Simiarly, Eliade (1964:27) writes " . . . the shaman is not only a sick man; he is above all a sick man who has been cured."

In a discussion of trance states and their psychopathology, cultural context is a very decisive element. That is, the shaman's trance cannot be abstracted from its cultural milieu. His mystical journeys and alternate personalities are not idiosyncratic; they do not isolate him from the community. The spirits who possess him and the worlds to which he travels are recognized by the community and are part and parcel of the belief system. At this juncture, the symbolic system is crucial, for the symbols brought forth in the shaman's trance must be both transformative for the shaman and empathic for his audience. The practicing shaman must adapt himself to the role expectations of the community. It is not enough that he has visions and enters into controlled trance states; he must give form to these states so they will serve the community. Indeed, this cultural embedding of the altered state of consciousness may in itself be an important means of discriminating pathological states from shamanism. Bourguignon (1976a: 38), referring to Haitian possession trance and its distinction from the type of dissociation found in multiple personality, writes:

> The great difference between such a patient and the characteristic Haitian cult initiate (or for that matter, a possession trancer in any of the 251 sample societies and many others as well) is that these (the multiple personality) dissociations are purely idiosyncratic; the behavior is not learned by following a cultural model. No one has attempted to teach dissociation to Sybil; to her associates it can only seem weird and bizarre and not the ordinary behavior of

> familiar and recognizable spirit entities. . . . In Haiti, dissociation into diverse (spirit) personalities fits in with the understanding people have of the universe, of gods and human nature.

Silverman (1967:25-26) and Wallace (1970:237-238) believe the shamanic experience to be pathological, but point up that cultural acceptance and validating labels for the experience distinguish it from other pathological experiences. Nevertheless, the questions of whether or not the shaman is pathological is not a simple one. Some researchers have administered Rorschach tests (Boyer *et al.* 1964; Gillin 1948; Lantis 1960), Holtzman ink blot techniques (Fabrega and Silver 1970) and other type of psychiatric examinations (Sasaki 1969), all with equivocal results. It may well be that the particular experiences a shaman undergoes include some that, by Western standards, are associated with neurosis or psychosis. However, interpretations differ. There are many reports of shamans with strong stable personalities who manifest no evidence of distorted episodes or deviance (Handleman 1967; Nadel 1965; M. K. Opler 1959). There is also evidence suggesting the opposite. For example, Firth (1967b: 295) reports that the medium for the principal Tikopian god had "periodic fits of craziness" and would at times "rush shrieking into the lake." But "even when mad he would, on the appropriate ritual occasions, enter into trance and behave in an organized manner. His psychic controls were evidently strong enough so that the social call of duty restored him to some equilibrium, from which he relapsed again after the rite was over." Thus there is no unequivocal answer; shamans as a group cannot be considered of one personality type any more than members of social or cultural groups.

I shall not adjudicate on whether shamans are ill or not, but will point out that the trance state experienced by the shaman during his ritual duties is in itself not pathological. Indeed, these so-called regressed states are very similar to certain forms of psychotherapy. In Tamang society, the initiatory process is systematic, with precise psychological goals and methods for attaining them. Apprenticeship is both didactic (myth and ritual, procedures and methods) and ecstatic (learning to master and use the trance). In a sense, the neophyte shaman, like the Western psychotherapist, receives a training analysis. And the training is not merely therapeutic for the shaman but also leads to acquisition of the shamanic vocation, the most important social function of which is community psychotherapist.

There is an important connection between training and social function. The latter involves the social employment of the ecstatic states mastered and controlled by the shaman. During apprenticeship, the shaman learns to master the spirits that possess him, and to dispatch and retrieve his soul, techniques which qualify him to heal his patients and disciples who suffer from the same afflictions he has overcome (i.e., spirit possession and soul loss). The purpose of this book is to illustrate the active elements in the Tamang process of shamanistic healing and initiation, and to account for the effectiveness of these practices in terms of Western psychology. This is, in other words, an ethnopsychiatric analysis of the practices and trance states of the Tamang shaman.

Shamanism and Healing

The shaman's role as community healer is well documented cross-culturally. Many studies have emphasized that the shaman's role as psychotherapist centers around his ability to treat social conflict. Lewis (1966:314-319; 1971:100 ff) considers that illnesses caused by "social deprivations," especially as a result of oppression at the hands of those politically more powerful, are treated most effectively by shamans in numerous societies. The theory sets forth that symptoms ranging from psychosomatic ailments to hysteria and depression are actually "oblique aggressive strategies" designed to extract redress from the socially dominant. In male-oriented societies, illness is used by women to protest against their husbands who must indicate concern by participating in healing rituals centered around the patient, where interpersonal conflicts are aired (see Chapter 7). Whether or not one accepts deprivation theory, the data clearly indicates that the shaman treats illness by treating social relations. An excellent example of this is the Ndembu "doctor" who sees his task less as curing than as remedying the ills of the corporate group (Turner 1964:262). Or, as Carstairs (1969:409) writes from his Indian experience, " . . . (the healer) reintegrates the mentally ill patient with the rest of the community from whom he has been estranged." (parenthesis mine). This is also the case among the Tamang, whose shamans are keen observers of social interrelations, frequenting the tea shops and taverns where local gossip abounds so that they can learn about potential clients' social problems. The information so obtained is used later in rituals that relieve social tension (Peters 1978, 1979).

As well as remedying social ills, the Tamang shaman's curing rituals bring about catharsis, rally group support around the patient, enhance suggestion and arouse faith and hope in the patient. These are major elements in all forms of psychotherapy, contemporary or "primitive" (Kennedy 1974:1177f).

The shaman can influence his patient's social relations and psychological valences because of the culturally shared religous faith attached to his ministrations. Levi-Strauss (1963:183-187) observed that traditional mythology functions in ritual as paradigm for the patient's pathological condition and treatment. He relates a myth told by the Cuna of Panama in which good triumphs over evil, and describes the patient's symbolic identification with the myth as effective psychotherapy. Similarly, Obeyesekere (1969:208) relates the ritual enactment of a Sinhalese myth by a healer and his assistants, where the conquest of demons becomes a metaphorical idiom through which healing occurs. As Malinowski (1926:21) put it, "Myth is not just a story told but a reality lived." The shaman places illness into the context of cultural beliefs, providing a rationale and meaning to the patient's otherwise chaotic and obscure distress, as well as a prescription for relief. The Tamang shaman accomplishes this from the context of the group's mythology which provides the scenario for a dramatic ritual reenactment through which the patient becomes identified with mythic prototypes and dominant cultural symbols of health and well-being. This movement from chaos to order within the context of myth and symbol marks a favorable direction in the healing process.

* * *

In Chapter 2, the socio-cultural context of Tamang shamanism is discussed so as to provide the cultural setting for proper perspective of the shaman's trance performances and initiations. Without this background, the shaman's beliefs might seem idiosyncratic, unrelated and removed from social reality. The general history, geography, and Tamang social organization and role in caste-conscious Nepal are examined.

The data presented here were obtained through a combination of field methods. As well as employing the traditional participant-observer type of field study, I attempted the experiential approach. In order to better understand the phenomenon being studied, an apprenticeship as a Tamang shaman was undertaken, and the ensuing trance states, visions, dreams, and treatments administered during a time of personal crisis are utilized as data. These experiences and the personal relationship with my key informant are discussed in Chapter 3.

The social role and functions of the shaman and other religious specialists in Tamang society are discussed in Chapter 4; Chapter 5 presents the world of spirits which is basic to Tamang religion and the shamanic medical system. It is this world of spirits which the shaman comes to master on behalf of his patients.

The final segment of the text is concerned with Tamang psychotherapy. Chapter 6 describes the four stages of initiation as they were described by the guru. The psychological aspects of these stages and the techniques used to produce them are then analyzed and compared to concepts of contemporary psychology and psychopathology. Chapter 7 details a Tamang curing ritual and outlines the shaman's healing practices; these are compared to contemporary psychotherapy in order to account for their effectiveness.

In the conclusion (Chapter 8), a synthesis of the diverse elements of the Tamang shamanistic complex is attempted. Comparisons are drawn between the "initiatory sickness" of the neophyte shaman and the patient's affliction, and their cures. In both, a psychological crisis is evoked and the same symbols are utilized to guide the individual's sentiments into socially valued pathways. This rechanneling of emotions is viewed as psychotherapeutic and is the main function of all Tamang curing and initiatory rituals. Thus the shamanistic practice of curing and of being cured is explored through experiential and more traditional participant-observation ethnographic field methods.

CHAPTER TWO

Tamang Culture in the Context of Nepalese Society

The Ethnographic Setting

Nepal,[1] a land-locked kingdom, is located on the southern slopes of the Himalayas. To its north lies Tibet (now part of the Peoples Republic of China); India lies to its south and west; Sikkim to the east. Lying as she does between the two great and ancient centers of civilization, India and China, Nepal has taken the political stance of a buffer state, dating back to the time of Prithvinarayan Shah (1730-1775). This Gorkha King conquered the three Malla kingdoms in the Kathmandu Valley. He was also the progenitor of a unification process which extended the domain of Nepal from the Valley to its present borders. He once described his kingdom as a "root between two stones." The policy of maintaining an independent nation, separate and apart from its neighbors, is the essence of Nepal's foreign policy (see Rose 1971).

Within Nepal live many ethnic groups. Turner (1927:65-6) lists three separate language families spoken among Nepal's inhabitants: Munda (a division of Austro-Asiatic), Tibeto-Burmese, and Indo-European. The Munda-speaking peoples are Nepal's oldest inhabitants. The Tibeto-Burmese-speaking peoples advanced into Nepal from Tibet and overlaid the indigenous inhabitants, becoming

[1] Nepal was originally just the Kathmandu Valley. The Buddhist *Vamśavali* texts, which are considered the oldest Nepalese literature, say that the Valley was called Nepal ("country cherished by Ne, the Sender to Paradise") (Hasrat 1970:7).

2. The towering Boudha *stupa*.
A lotus design adorns its whitewashed tumulus and Buddha-eyes painted at the base of its spire look out in all four directions.

the most numerous population of Nepal. The Tamang speak a Tibeto-Burmese language and constitute the largest ethnic minority (pop. 518,812) in Nepal, a country of perhaps 13 million (Bista 1967:XI,32,52).[2] The Indo-European speakers came to Nepal most recently of the three groups, but it is their language which is the most widely spoken. Nepali (closely related to Hindi) is the language of the Gorkha rulers and the official language of the country. Further, it is the *lingua franca* of the Kathmandu Valley, and was spoken by the Tamang in Boudha and Tin Chuli, located less than five miles from Kathmandu, where field work was conducted in 1976 and 1977.

Most Tamang live in the Bagmati Zone.[3] There are 25,000 or so in the Kathmandu Valley itself and, except for perhaps 20,000 in the newly-settled Terai (a tropical jungle area), the remainder live in the hills below 8,000 feet to the east and west of the Valley. Different dialects of Tamang are spoken by the people in the western and eastern hills and in the Valley, and there are probably variations in between. My field assistant was born and raised in the Kathmandu Valley and his first language was Tamang; yet he was unable to communicate in either eastern or western Tamang dialects.

It may well be that the geography of Nepal plays a major role in the divergence of language and other cultural features. Nepal is a country of towering mountains and deep valleys that do not permit easy communication; nor are they conducive to unification. Footpaths are the only links between villages; roads, telephone, telegraph, electricity were virtually nonexistent outside of the Kathmandu Valley and Pokhara in 1977.

Nepal is essentially an agricultural country; agriculture and related endeavors currently account for about 63% of its economy

[2] Frank (1974:94) also considers the Tamang to be Nepal's largest ethnic group. He counted 511,420 in his research area which consisted of all of Nepal except for the five outer Terai districts between Chitwan and Danussha.

[3] Nepal is divided into 14 zones, comprising 75 districts. Bagmati Zone is the central zone; within its perimeter is the Kathmandu Valley.

(Stiller 1976:13). That percentage is certainly higher among Tamang. In Boudha, which is an acculturated bazaar town, my own survey showed that 72.1% of the Tamang are engaged in agricultural endeavors. And, in Tin Chuli, located just ¼ mile north of Boudha, a more rural Tamang village, nearly 100% are farmers, although many villagers supplement this by carrying loads or performing other labor.

The great Malla ruler, Jayasthiti Malla (died 1395) is usually credited as being the man who "codified the whole structure of Nepalese society in a strictly orthodox Hindu frame," (Hasrat 1970:xlii). The present-day Shah rulers of Nepal are from the Chetri (Skt: Kshatriya) or warrior caste. They and the Brahmans (priests) are the highest castes. Turner (1927:65-66) gives a listing of caste ranking which includes the Tibeto-Burmese speakers as well. The Tamang (or Murmi)[4] are ranked next to the lowest, above the Tharu (inhabitants of the Terai). Northey and Morris (1927:259) write, "While the exact social status of the Murmi is not easy to define, it is certainly below that of the Magar, Gurung, Limbu, Rai and Sunwar, and the men of these tribes would always consider themselves superior to them." Fürer-Haimendorf (1978:15) notes that Tamang social position is low; they may only enter Chetri households in the capacity of servants and farmhands. In the Tamang society of Boudha and Tin Chuli, the Tamang were considered socially superior only to the outcaste occupational groups (e.g., shoemaker, tailor, butcher).

A commonly known myth relates that the Tamang are descended from the great god Mahesur (or Śiva), who was tricked into eating a cow by his elder brothers, Brahma and Vishnu. When he realized his shame, Śiva became enraged and threw the cow's entrails at his brothers, some of which stuck around their shoulders. This is said to account for why Hindus wear the sacred

[4] Tamang were sometimes called Murmi or Lama in the early literature (Northey and Morris 1927:256; Landon 1928 II:246). These names may be in current use among Tamang living in Darjeeling district (Fürer-Haimendorf 1956:166,n.2). Many of my informants were introduced to me as Mr. Lama. However, they were not priests but called themselves Lama because it is a term of respect that creates a favorable impression.

thread. The myth is also used to explain why most Tamang eat beef freely. In Nepal, which is a sacred Hindu state, they have to wait for the animal to die first, since killing the sacred beast is both unthinkable and punishable. The identification as carrion-eaters is often used by Tamang and others to explain their low status in Nepalese society. Being called a cow-eater in Nepal is one of the worst things one person could say about another.[5]

It is not my objective to enter into the problems of the Nepalese caste system; it is an extremely complicated subject that needs much more research. However, caste is generally adhered to and has numerous effects, the most noticeable being that it is an active force segregating ethnic groups, while simultaneously promoting intragroup solidarity.

Tamang distinguish themselves from other groups by the word *jat* (caste), but the strict sense of the word (occupational group) is not applicable except for the outcastes. Many Brahman, Chetri, Tamang, and others are engaged in subsistence farming. Institutional factors (endogamy, commensality, hierarchy), more than economic factors, maintain caste distinctions.

Given these circumstances, Tamang have little representation in top-level government jobs. F. H. Gaige (1975:166-169) gives a statistical breakdown of national-level administrative jobs in 1969 which shows that all hill peoples (Tamang, Gurung, Magar, Rai, Limbu and Sherpa) had a total of 5.3%, or 9 out of 170 positions. In the 1967 "Caste Breakdown Among Senior Army Officers," there were only 2 Tamang officers. Tamang in the army generally serve as tent pitchers and heavy load carriers. The vast majority of army officers are, of course, of Chetri caste.

Widespread illiteracy among Tamang is a primary contributor to their participatory absence in Nepali government. In order to hold elected office above the village level, one must be literate.

[5] In *An Account of the Kingdom of Nepal*, Hamilton (1819) writes: "The doctrine of the *lama* is so obnoxious to the Gorkhalese that, under pretense of their being thieves, no Murmi is permitted to enter the Valley where Kathmandu stands, and by way of ridicule they are called Siyenu Bhotiyas, or Bhotiyas who eat carrion." (quoted in Macdonald 1975a:144).

3. The main street of Boudha,
the road that connects it with Kathmandu, three miles southeast.
The open trench at right serves as the village sewer system.

UNICEF (1975:10) gave Nepali literacy rates (1971) as 14% (up from 5% in 1951); women's literacy rates lag at 3.9%. Based on my own observations, the Tamang literacy rate is substantially below the national averages.

Nepal is a poor and developing nation. Sanitation is absent, disease ever-present, infant mortality 15%-20%, and average life expectancy is only 40.6 years (UNICEF 1974). The Tamang are one of Nepal's poorest ethnic groups.

The Village of Boudha

Boudha is a large bazaar town of 2,012 people.[6] In 160 households (1,690 people), almost 60% are Tamang. The other major population groups are Tibetans[7] and Newars. Most Tibetans are refugees from the 1959 invasion of Tibet by the Chinese. Many shopkeepers on the bazaar line are Newars. Of the Newar, 1.3% of families are engaged in farming, compared to 72.1% among the Tamang. The majority of the Newars are shopkeepers (53.7%), gold and silversmiths (12%). The Tibetans are primarily rug weavers or *thanka* (Tib: sacred scroll) painters (41%), shopkeepers (24.3%) and monks (22.3%). Thus the Newars and Tibetans are the shopkeepers and artisans; the Tamang the farmers.

Boudha is a famous pilgrimage site. The glittering spire of its enormous reliquary tumulus (*stupa*) can be seen from vantages all over the Valley. Thousands of pilgrims visit annually from India as well as Nepal, and thousands more used to come from Tibet and China. Hardly a full moon passes without a festival taking place around the *stupa*.

The *stupa* brings an air of numinosity to the village, as anyone who has seen the throngs making daily circumambulation and prostration around it could support. The faithful circle around

[6] October 1976, personal survey.

[7] Tibetans, Tamang, and other tribes of Tibetan descent (Magar, Gurung, *et al.*) are called "Bhota" (Tib: *böd-pa*, "one from Tibet"). (Also see note 5 above.)

the *stupa* counting their rosary beads; some hold prayer wheels but most turn the large brass prayer cylinders recessed in the white octagonal walls surrounding the *stupa*. All chant "OM MANI PADME HUM." Two Tibetan monasteries are located on the *stupa*'s periphery; another two are a few feet beyond. In all, 124 monks (almost all Tibetan)[8] comprise a visible red-robed presence.

In the dwellings that immediately surround the *stupa* live 430 people, not counting the 25-30 Western "enlightenment-seekers" who study at the monasteries and constitute a regular transient population. During the day, women work winnowing their grain, nursing their children, chopping wood for their cook-stoves, weaving straw mats, washing dishes, picking nits, rubbing each other with oil, all on the pavement around the *stupa*. Men gamble at cards, shells and dice. Children play marbles. The concrete pavement slabs are dotted with holes that serve as the children's latrines. The pariah dogs clean up whatever is left behind .

The *stupa* is known by two names: Kasha Chait in Nepali, Jarung Khasor in Tibetan. Oldfield (1880 II:261) relates that the *stupa* was named after a great Tibetan *lama* named Kasha who died in Nepal while on pilgrimage; the *stupa* was ostensibly erected as a receptacle for his ashes. But in *The Legend of the Great Stupa* (1973:28), a translation of a Tibetan *terma* text (i.e., authorship attributed to Padma Sambhava who is credited with bringing Buddhism to Tibet), the *stupa* is said to be a reliquary for Maha-kashyapa, the Buddha of the age before Sakyamuni. The *terma* text also accounts for the second name. The story of the *stupa* is common knowledge in Boudha and Tin Chuli. The myth reported here is the one collected in the field, which is a little different from the published account:

[8] There is only one Tamang monk in the monasteries. The Tamang and Tibetans generally maintain different practices, and worship at different places. The Tamang "monastery" has no resident *lama* and so is really a temple containing many beautiful icons and scrolls. The Tamang *lama* do not wear robes, although they sometimes don a red and white shawl on important ritual occasions.

> It is said that the little daughter of King Indra stole some flowers from his garden and was punished by being reborn on Earth as a daughter of a poultry man. Her name was Shamvara. When she matured, she became a whore and copulated with four men of low caste, and had four child-dren by them. After accumulating much wealth, she decided to repent for her sins and build a *stupa*. Going to the great Buddhist King of Tibet, Srong Tsen Gampo (reigned 620-649 A.D.), she asked permission to build a *stupa* that would cover only as much land as a buffalo hide.[9] The king could not refuse such a small request, and replied "*jarung*," which means "proceed with the work." Before starting work, Shamvara cut the whole buffalo hide around and around as thin as a piece of thread. Stretching out the thread, it equaled the circumference of the Boudha *stupa*. The people complained to the king, saying that the *stupa* was too big and took up land that could be used to better purpose. But the king was a man of his word, so he said, "*jarung khasor*" which means "I have already given my permission to proceed with the work."

The story ends by telling of the future incarnations of Shamvara's four sons. One became the famous Buddhist scholar who intro-duced the alphabet into Tibet, Thonmi Sambhota. The second son became the lotus guru, Padma Sambhava (Guru Rinpoche). Another son cursed the amount of work he had to do and was reborn as the wicked king Lang Dharma, whom Waddell (1894:34) called the "Julian of Lamaism." The fourth son was reborn as Lhalung Paldorje, the monk who killed Lang Dharma and saved Buddhism in Tibet.[10]

Many Tamang believe that Shamvara was an incarnation of Ajima, whose shrine is the largest at the *stupa* and located directly opposite the Tamang monastery. Ajima is Boudha's territorial

[9] The hide part of the myth is not contained in the *terma* text.

[10] The story of the sons' reincarnations is not matched in the *terma* text but the other elements of the story are the same (also see Landon 1928 I:202-204).

4. The house of the Chinea lama, as seen from the Boudha *stupa*.
To the left of the house is the small Tamang temple.
A larger Tibetan monastery lies surrounded by rice paddies beyond.

deity, charged by Padma Sambhava with the protection of the people of Boudha.

The *stupa*'s exact age is not known. However, S. Levi (as quoted in Landon 1928 I:198) suggests that the Boudha *stupa* dates back to the reign of Mana Deva (496-512 A.D.).

According to my informants, until 50 years ago the area around the *stupa* was considered a sanctuary for criminals fleeing the Nepalese authorities. They needed only to have permission from the *lama* presiding over the *stupa* (see Hasrat 1970:30,n.1). Going to the *stupa* for refuge was like going to Tibet. Thus Boudha came to be known as "Little Tibet."

The Chinea Lama

The present-day abbot of the Tamang monastery, and guru to most of the Boudha Tamang *lama*, is the Chinea Lama (lit: Chinese Lama). He is the richest and most powerful man in the village. According to the Chinea Lama, his family has been in charge of the *stupa* since 1872 when Ty Fu Sing, the first Chinea Lama, came from China to Nepal. According to differing stories, Ty Fu was either appointed by the Chinese Emperor to be his representative at the Nepalese court, or summoned by Prime Minister Jung Bahadur Rana. In any event, the powerful Prime Minister asked the Chinese noble to tutor his grandson in Chinese. In time he was given charge over the Boudha *stupa* and other major shrines (including the ancient *stupa* at Swayambu and Lumbini, Buddha's birthplace). He was also given thousands of hectars of *guthi* land, non-taxable farmland which supports the Chinea Lama, his family, the *stupa*, its maintenance, and annual celebrations.[11]

Legend has it that Jung Bahadur Rana gave Ty Fu Sing his favorite concubine to marry. She was a wealthy Tamang girl, the

[11] The deed to the Chinea Lama's *guthi* land is on a *sanak putra* (lit: written authority) bearing the seal of King Prithvi Bir Vikram Shah (reigned 1881-1911). Several informants claimed to have seen it, but I never did.

daughter of a hereditary *lama*.[12] Taking a Tamang wife was certainly a political advantage. The abbott of the Boudha *stupa* is both the official ambassador of the Dalai Lama, and the head of the Tamang Buddhist community. Their eldest son would inherit the position of Chinea Lama. Jung Bahadur Rana was no doubt pleased to have a man he trusted governing this Bhote community since Nepal had been at war with Tibet twice in less than 100 years (1788 and 1854).

The current Chinea Lama has ten Tamang disciples. Their main responsibility is to officiate at funeral ceremonies, playing music and reading from *The Tibetan Book of the Dead*. Tamang *lama* are of the Nyingma sect of Tibetan Buddhism. They are not required to be celibate, and some enter into polygynous marriages. Some of the Chinea Lama's disciples are businessmen, one is a politician, another a well-to-do farmer. The Chinea Lama himself is a very wealthy man. Aside from his considerable *guthi* holdings, he is a broker and exporter of Tibetan painted scrolls and carpets, employing many of the Tamang and Tibetan craftsmen in the area.

The Chinea Lama's house and curio shop adjoin the Tamang monastery. Some 87 of the Chinea Lama's children, grandchildren, and great-grandchildren live either in his house or others he provides. The two men who served as my field assistants during my year in Boudha are grandsons, and my family and I lived on land owned by the Chinea Lama's youngest son.

[12] According to the Chinea Lama and one other of my *lama* informants, there are six hereditary Tamang *lama* clans (Nyima Hoesar, Sakya Shangbo, Sampatta, Guram Syumba, Lhalung Pal Dorje, and Dhimi Ngi Dong). However, none of the Western writers on Tamang culture mention *lama* clans (see Fürer-Haimendorf 1956:177), and they do not exist in Boudha or Tin Chuli, except for the Chinea Lama's family. They are said to exist in Rasua and northern Dhading districts, in the Tamang villages of Bhren Dang, Ghandar Chu, and Sertong. The Chinea Lama says his grandmother, Ty Fu Sing's Tamang wife, was from the Sampatta clan living in Bhren Dang.

5. The village of Tin Chuli, separated from Boudha by fields and terraces.

A typical Tamang house in Tin Chuli. In the center of the yard is a thatched
ructure on four stilts in which grain is stored. The pot on its top keeps the birds
om breaking in. When hollowed out and erected in a cemetery, this structure
ecomes a *qufa*, used during a shaman's final initiation.

The Village of Tin Chuli

As mentioned earlier, Tin Chuli is about ¼ mile behind (north) Boudha. There are 360 people in 63 households living there, almost all of whom (lacking only 3 households) are farmers. All but 5 households are Tamang. There are another 24 Tamang households in Arubari, the larger Chetri farming village adjacent to Tin Chuli.

Tin means three and *chuli* oven. Cooking in Nepal is traditionally done on stoves comprised of three stones depicting a triangle. The fire is set between the stones and the cooking utensil placed on top. In the center of Tin Chuli are three large stones set up under a pipal tree (*ficus religiosa*). It is said to be the oven used to cook the food of the workers who built the great *stupa*.

With few exceptions, the farmers of Tin Chuli are tenants on *birtha* and *guthi* land. *Guthi* land has already been explained; *birtha* land is awarded in return for services to the crown, often to high-ranking army officers or top-level bureaucrats. Under *birtha* and *guthi* systems, the tenants pay 50% of their annual harvests to the landlords. Failure to pay can lead to eviction. Bhirendra, my key informant, is a tenant on Tin Chuli *guthi* land.[13]

Tin Chuli is bound to Boudha in many ways. In the larger village are the mills and bazaar. They are tied religiously as well, celebrating their common beliefs during the four major festivals held annually at the Boudha *stupa*.

The Village Shamans

The Tamang shamans of Boudha and Tin Chuli are independent of one another; there is no organization or group of shamans.

[13] See Stiller (1976) and Regmi (1963-8; 1971; 1976) for more complete explanations of the land tenure systems and the plight of the peasant in Nepal's history.

Since they are highly competitive and suspicious of one another, only the guru/disciple relationship brings two together. This is the only way in which information or doctrine is communicated. However, the area *bombo* were more relaxed with each other than with outsiders. Bhirendra sometimes borrowed bells or drums for his disciples from one of the Boudha *bombo*. But to my knowledge, they never "talked shop." When a coincidental meeting between unacquainted *bombo* occurred, it was generally short and sharp, sometimes characterized by a boasting duel. If a *bombo* shows fear, his foe can cause him to fall ill or even die by virtue of his greater power (*śakti*).

So it is easy to understand why shamanic systems differ. Even when information is passed on from guru to disciple, there is room for wide divergence (see Macdonald 1976a:326). However, my three main informants, each coming from a different Tamang village, employed essentially the same shamanic system.

While I worked closest with Bhirendra, there were at least eight other shamans in the area. Bhirendra was clearly the most informed and was regarded by the villagers as being the *thulo bombo* (big shaman).

At times, the Boudha villagers called on shamans from outside the area. One *bombo*, from a village in East #1 district about 25 miles away, was called into Boudha once every few weeks. He would spend three or four days and perform as many healing rituals. He became one of my better informants and we discussed in depth his *puja*, cosmology, and shamanism in general.

Another of my shaman informants came from Mulkarka, located three hours walk from Boudha in the mountains just east of the Kathmandu Valley. We met when I was searching out potential field sites. Although I did not choose to settle in Mulkarka, I was impressed by the shaman's knowledge in our first interview. Later, I attended several of his *puja*, and he stopped by my house whenever he came into Kathmandu. Both the Mulkarka and East #1 shamans provided excellent sources of comparison for Bhirendra's system; the three were in agreement on almost all essentials.

Because each of these *bombo* lived some distance away from

each other, the system revealed represents a fairly extensive cultural tradition, one quite different from what has been published on Tamang shamanism to date (Höfer 1974). Höfer's account, however, deals with Tamang living west of the Valley, whereas my informants were raised in areas east of the Valley.

CHAPTER THREE

The Experiential Study of Tamang Shamanism

The spectrum of anthropological fieldwork ranges from "unobtrusive measures" (Webb, Campbell, Schwartz and Sechrest 1966) and techniques of "direct observation" which demand investigator objectivity, to the more subjectively involved "complete participation" (Junker 1960). Commenting on the value of the participatory aspect of fieldwork, Pelto and Pelto (1978:69) write " . . . it is difficult to overestimate the importance of the information that the anthropologist accumulates through direct participation." This type of field role has also been found effective in the study of religious systems and altered states of consciousness (Jules-Rosette 1973; Maquet 1975; Staal 1975; Tart 1972). Because my research involved the study of both a religious system and the trance states which are its most salient characteristic, an attempt was made to experience these, believing that a more complete knowledge would result if I experienced what my informants said they did. Accordingly, certain phases of research involved participation and introspection.

The "experiential approach," according to Maquet (1978: 362-363), " . . . is the investigator's awareness of his own inner reactions when going through a patterned behavioral process in another culture or subculture. This makes possible direct observation of some mental states, and helps to constitute a body of references for communication with other persons undergoing a similar experience." Thus, while the experiential method demands a direct participation in the system of beliefs and practices of the culture being studied, it is not the same thing as

7. An initiation ceremony for the disciple shamans conducted during a pilgrimage.

"going native." The latter is more appropriately associated with a conversion to another belief system and the absence of a critical perspective. The experiential method demands a combination of talents–scholar as well as disciple.

The experiential method is not exclusively "emic" or "etic" but synthesizes elements of both. It demands intimate knowledge of the cultural categories by which experiences are interpreted and described by the people under study, as well as a discursive perspective. Yet, it differs from other approaches in that it is always participatory and introspective, utilizing the experiences and self-observations of the ethnographer as viable tools of research.

In the experiential approach employed by Maquet (1975, 1980) in his study of Buddhist meditation in Sri Lanka, the anthropologist became a member of the in-group and was thus able to observe his own inner states while going through an indigenous cultural practice designed to produce certain mental states. He then reported and interpreted these experiences for an academic audience.

Jules-Rosette (1978:553-556) describes a similar experiential "folk inquiry" comprised of a four-fold process in which the investigator moves from initial "conceptions" of the other thought system; to "discovery" which is an "exchange of subjective positions" in order to experience what is being studied as a member; this is followed by the development of an analytical stance for "evaluation"; and finally there is "communication" to those who have not undergone the immersion experience, in a language that merges experience and abstraction.

There are various levels of participation within the experiential approach. Maquet (1975:182) and Jules Rosette (1976:132ff) represent examples of one extreme in that they both professed a personal commitment to religious doctrine. A more limited approach is the "introspective ethnography" used by Riesman (1977:2,149) who reports that once he had integrated himself fully into the life shared by the Fulani of West Africa, they behaved toward him as toward each other. Yet a whole side of him escaped their attention (i.e., everything Western, including the need to gather data for a thesis) and these factors influenced his thoughts and sensitivities, causing him to react differently than they to certain incidents. Riesman participated simultaneously in two cultural systems, and each affected him differently. Another example of this more limited experiential approach comes from Ridington (1969) who suggests a "symbolic transformation" of the ethnographer so that he can experience reality from the conceptual standpoint of his informants, but which stops short of cultural conversion. Similarly, Staal (1975:130) and Tart (1972:1207) both approach the study of mystical states by recommending that the investigator first adopt an uncritical attitude, to be replaced at some point by scientific perspective.

My personal circumstances, biases and lifestyle made it impossible to carry out a complete participatory inquiry. The "permeability of realities" described by ethnomethodologists (Mehan and Wood 1975:27f) was never completely experienced. I did not undergo religious or cultural conversion to the Tamang belief system, but I did take a guru with whom a relationship was developed that eventually transcended cultural barriers and intellectual biases, thereby enabling me to experience Tamang shamanism and ecstasy as an apprentice.

Choosing the Guru

Bhirendra, my guru and key informant, is 45 years old, and shamanism provides him with supplemental income to farming, the principal means by which he supports his wife, parents, and four children. By all standards, he is a typical Tamang man, except that he is a philosopher of his culture—a man who has given a lot of thought to the world and the beliefs that serve as its charter. I was immediately impressed with his knowledge of Tamang mythology; at our first meeting, he recounted the cosmology and anthropogeny myths in much more detail than the three other shamans who had been interviewed earlier. He spoke with conviction, and his rituals were dramatic and compelling affairs lasting from dusk to dawn (Peters 1978).

I explained that I had come from America to learn his methods of healing so that they could be shared with colleagues and serve others. He readily agreed and showed immediate concern about how much he would get paid for the information. Terms were negotiated; meetings four times a week and an invitation to all the rituals he performed. Bhirendra wanted a week's advance as a show of faith. I complied and did not see him again for two weeks. He vanished completely and I suspect his wife and parents lied to me when I came looking for him. Throughout our relationship, advances were always a mistake. Money in pocket, Bhirendra would disappear on journeys or binges that would last as long as the money held out.

Fieldwork was not restricted to the experiential approach and other methods were utilized to gather data dealing with the socio-cultural context of ecstasy. It was immediately apparent that the shaman's trance did not exist of and for itself but was restricted to specific ceremonies, particularly healing rituals. From the beginning, interviews with Bhirendra focused on recording the magical and animistic healing beliefs. Interviews were also conducted with villagers in order to accumulate needed information. Living in the village, observing the daily activities, I was able to witness the shamans' role within the context of community life. Once my presence was accepted, friendships were formed. I was invited to attend numerous healing rituals and conducted follow-up interviews with patients. The Tamang were generally very friendly and open.

As time passed, it became apparent that Bhirendra was a highly effective healer. I became personally fond of him although this wasn't the case early on. He is a trickster-type character, and many of his ways of doing things are contrary to what I had expected. Still, he is dedicated to his patients and shows real compassion for their ills, charging each what he feels they can afford. He often haggles with his patients over the cost of a ritual; but if necessary he performs it free of charge (albeit less elaborately). Outside of his noble role as community doctor, he is a bit of a scoundrel. He was in my bedroom one day when we returned from a family outing. He explained that he wanted to see what was up there, but I suspected he might be selecting something.

I had to be up and out of the house before dawn each day if our meetings were to occur. Even so, he often left earlier for the tavern. He had reasons for going there outside of his obvious fondness for alcohol, one being that the tavern is a village meeting place where much personal gossip is exchanged. It is the perfect place for a shaman to pick up news about family conflicts and the like, information which he repeated during his diagnostic rituals when the spirits possessed him. Bhirendra also liked to show his drinking buddies how the Western "professor" chased after him, a situation which definitely elevated his stature. Each time he took money and then disappeared, it seemed that his sense of one-upmanship outweighed the importance of the wages lost.

Tamang shamans are suspicious rivals. Shamanic knowledge passes only from guru to disciple, never between shamans. Under most circumstances, the shamans try to avoid one another. Should rivals meet, a verbal duel for supremacy immediately ensues, one boasting of his exploits, the other of his powerful *mantra* (magical formulae). They are afraid to eat together and protect themselves against poisoning by passing special hand gestures over their food. There are numerous stories about shamans powerful enough to kill with their supernatural powers. Bhirendra claimed to know how to do this and more; he promised to protect all of his disciples from spells and "psychic arrows" of rival practitioners.

Only once did I observe two shamans working together. One of the first rituals I attended was for a family who had recently moved to Boudha. They called a shaman from their former village to cure the woman of the house. This shaman later became one of my informants. On this occasion, he showed up with a "partner." The day after the ritual, the shamans stopped at my house for an interview and we discussed the preceding evening's events. They offered to sell 36 myths they said comprised the "complete" (oral) Ta: *bombo sherab*, or "shaman's wisdom." They seemed knowledgeable so we agreed on a price and got to work. They failed to deliver all they had promised and we argued before compromising on a sum which was picked up the next morning by the shaman's cohort. Shortly thereafter, the shaman arrived and asked for his money. I suspected subterfuge at first, but by mid-morning it was apparent that the shaman had been swindled by his associate.

Despite the many things that separated me from Bhirendra, I respected his religious endeavor and valued his keen mind and amazing memory. He was a rich source of knowledge that could be confirmed and validated by other shamans. My admiration for his important role in the community was a major bond between us, and our friendship was based on more than the boost given his status and wealth. After I became his disciple, he was consulted in more cases and his fame spread far beyond our community. Tavern keepers extended him credit, which he substantially abused. In a sense, he became middle class for a while. When he realized my stay was finite, our relationship became important to him and he embraced me as his friend.

As a guru, Bhirendra was an excellent choice. In the beginning, when our relationship was strictly business, he frequently embarrassed me in front of his friends to show off his superiority. After I had injured my knee trekking, he came to my house with several companions and told me to take off my pants so that he could heal it. I offered to roll up my pants but he demanded my obedience to make me prove my faith. He went to great lengths to assert his dominance in our relationship. Sometimes I would come home frustrated after a day searching for him, yelling that I was "through with that . . . ." The next morning, he would send someone to fetch me for teachings and I would swallow anger and pride and go after him.

Bhirendra is a great shaman and he cured numerous patients in my presence. He could induce "possession" and highly emotional states in his patients, in order to exorcise spirits. He performed breathtaking feats like immersing his hands in boiling oil and swallowing live coals. And he was awesome when possessed by the spirits. Highly accomplished as a musician and raconteur, he served as guru to six disciples including me, and, as mentioned before, was generally acknowledged to be the "big shaman" in the area. In time, he told me about his life and calling and initiated me into the secrets of his vocation.

8. A purification ritual (*silba puja*)
in which the author participated as a disciple shaman.

Taking the Guru

After he agreed to take me as a disciple, Bhirendra took four months before beginning my teachings. After ignoring my persistent wishes to become a shaman, he walked into my house one morning and announced that he had scheduled a purification rite for that evening in order to determine whether or not the gods would come to possess me. The time had come! Bhirendra and two disciples began the ritual that evening by lighting incense and chanting *mantra*. When it was time to "call on the gods," Bhirendra handed me a drum[1] and told me to play along. We sat cross-legged on the floor, holding the drum handles in our left hands and S-shaped drumsticks in our right, we all beat drums softly in a distinct 3-3 pattern. After a short time, the beat increased and the pattern was replaced by hard, extremely rapid strokes. The beating continued for several minutes but nothing happened to me. The exercise was repeated twice more; still nothing happened to me while Bhirendra and his disciples shook furiously. One disciple became possessed by his grandfather. His legs shook; then the trembling increased and spread through his body. At the height of their paroxysms, Bhirendra and the others were bounding two feet off the ground from their cross-legged positions, all the while smashing their drums at the hard, rapid pace.

We repeated the exercise again and again; I started to shake consciously and gradually I began letting go, becoming part of

[1] The *bombo* drums are approximately 15" in diameter, fashioned of goatskin over wood, with a carved wooden handle approximately 10" long. Neher (1961, 1962) has shown that, in laboratory conditions, auditory stimulus with a drum, beat at three, four, six and then eight cycles per second, as tested in a series of forty-second sessions separated by forty-second rest period, will produce the same effect on a subject as the rhythmic stimulation with bright light known as "photic driving" (see Walter 1953); that is, kinesthetic sensations such as swaying and spinning, and feeling states such as fear, disgust, confusion and fatigue. Finally, myoclonic jerks may appear, and a full-blown *grand mal* seizure may develop. Neher hypothesizes that there may be a connection between drum beating and the production of trance states (also see Prince 1968).

the beat itself. After a dozen or more times, the shaking in my legs became more automatic. They shook by themselves yet I was aware of this "non-doing." After a few moments, my whole body began to shake and I bounced all over the room. My attention was focused on my body movements and my eyes were closed. But as soon as I became aware of my surroundings, that other things were going on around me, the shaking ceased being automatic and subsided into fatigue.

Looking back on the drumming that night, it seems we played as fast as possible, everyone playing the same rhythm, bam-bam-bam, bam-bam-bam, in threes until the beating became even faster. The trembling seemed to evolve from conscious to automatic at the moment Bhirendra inserted a loud extra beat between two of mine, changing the rhythm and causing it to quicken. I'm sure he did this purposely and always used this method with his disciples. He made two or three of these drumming maneuvers before my drumming and shaking became automatic. At one point, my shaking continued until I felt a fleeting fear that I was losing control and being overwhelmed, at which point I became aware of my body trembling. It was a disturbing feeling, not very traumatic but nonetheless jolting. Afterwards, my heart pounded and I reasoned that my resistances were strong against surrendering to the experience. I hadn't fully "let go."

The first time I shook, Bhirendra and the other disciples were certain I had been chosen by a god to become a shaman. Bhirendra was proud of me and himself. "After all," he boasted, "I called on the gods." That evening they gave me a Nepalese nickname: *Sahib jhankri* (gentleman shaman). Villagers were drawn to my house by the drumming during the ritual, and by the next morning the entire village knew about my "possession."

Yet I felt no alien power enter me. I lost control of my movements and became scared; nothing else happened. Introspectively, I lost sense of time and surroundings, but my trance (if that is the proper term) was extremely light. Bhirendra and the other disciples thought I had been possessed. Because I had not progressed very far in my initiatory accomplishments, it was natural that I didn't know who had possessed me, nor had the god spoken through me, nor had there been visions.

My viewpoint differed. I did not believe I had been possessed. Bhirendra interpreted my shaking and fast drumming to the possession, my fear as fear of the deity—something he expected to occur in a neophyte. I saw the drum as a method to produce an altered state indigenously interpreted as possession, in my case a hyperactive automatic state with feelings of anxiety that was experientially different from normal waking consciousness. Bourguignon (1976a:8) writes that spirit possession occurs only in societies where people believe in it. Spirit possession could not exist for me because I don't hold the same animistic beliefs as my informants. Still I did experience something subjectively unusual.

The first purification rite was followed on subsequent nights by two equally exhausting sessions. But these were not as successful as the first. I explained my critical view of possession to Bhirendra who dismissed it saying, "You are new in this country; how do you know what exists here?" Up to that time, I had been in Nepal seven months learning about spirits that cause every type of misfortune. Still, I could neither accept the belief that spirits cause illness nor that I had been possessed by a spirit that night. Skepticism must have contributed to the failure of the subsequent two rituals in which I was unable to let myself go. I would begin shaking and become aware of the energy moving upwards. When the shaking reached my shoulders and neck, I stiffened and was unable to loosen up as I had the first night. This "stiffness of neck" was upsetting, symbolic of the inflexibility of my cultural biases. I told Bhirendra about my neck; he said I was afraid to let the god speak through me because I thought it would talk nonsense, and advised me not to let the thought bother me. At all of these purification rituals, Bhirendra was intent on having the gods speak through me, but he gave me no personal instruction regarding how to evoke this. Once he called on my father and grandfather (both deceased) while I was playing the drum and shaking, hoping he would have more success calling on my ancestors because they were closer to me than were the Nepali spirits. The spirits remained silent.

Undiscouraged, Bhirendra planned a pilgrimage for all the disciples to a special festival where shamans from all over Nepal bring their apprentices to help them advance beyond the first initiatory stages. He said we would dance together to Richeswar (40 miles south of Kathmandu) where the festival is held annually during the full moon of April. There we would pay homage to the Hindu god, Śiva, and gain his favor so that the gods would possess us and make us powerful shamans.

The festival at Richeswar fulfilled a long desired ambition: to go to a *bombo* festival as a participant! Despite my doubts about Śiva and the other gods and spirits, I had really experienced something on the night of the first ritual, and I wanted access to it again. With enthusiasm and determination, I threw myself into preparation for the festival.

At Bhirendra's instruction, a shaman's frock was tailored for me consisting of a white skirt, white Nepali shirt, red and white scarves to wrap around the head, and a peacock-feather headdress set in a gold and red headband. Bhirendra gave me a gift of a rosary of 108 black wooden beads special to the shamans, and lent me a string of bells.

The Initiation

Bhirendra, four other disciples and I met early the morning of the Richeswar pilgrimage. We donned our robes, secured each other's bells and feathers and, playing on our drums, left the house singing the traditional pilgrimage songs. We marched and drummed through our village to the jeep that would take us to Richeswar. Like many others from Kathmandu, we opted to go by motor. We stopped in every little village or group of houses where offerings had been left for us, and sang and danced the pilgrimage dance.

For days, we had been practicing the pilgrimage song, dance and drum accompaniment. Bhirendra explained the symbolism of the dance and the purpose of the pilgrimage: some came for initiation and blessing, others to be healed.

The villagers turned out to watch us leave for the pilgrimage; we danced down the main street and around the *stupa*. I was self-conscious in my colorful costume; my long skirt tripped me as I danced. An air of sanctity hung over the pilgrimage group. Along the way, there would be much joking and drinking, but when the *bombo* danced and sang, they were serious about their holy mission. From the moment we donned our robes, we had been transported from secular to sacred. Bhirendra said we were closer to the gods on the pilgrimage and that was why it was auspicious for initiations.

We found shelter in a half-finished barn at Richeswar that night. A few hundred people had made the pilgrimage, including several groups of shamans with their disciples. One group danced in front of our shelter. Bhirendra said they were only fair, and told us we were much better. We ate rice and drank *raksi*, the local liquor. Then we all sat down together and began a purification ritual.

The evening was spectacular; a million stars lit the sky that seemed near enough to touch from our Himalayan vantage. Outside our shelter, other groups drummed and sang. Dressed in our regalia, we were intent on the evening's initiation. We played and sang the sacred stories. During the singing, I began to sway back and forth, my headdress bobbed and bells jingled to the time of the music. I was filled with feelings of kinship for my brother initiates and especially my guru.

Bhirendra took complete charge of the ritual; setting the pace, his drumming echoed against the walls. I followed his beat. While my body was swaying, I lost myself in the music and began to shake. Bhirendra broke my pattern by inserting an extra beat or two in the rhythm, and my beating quickened. He repeated this three or four times and then I lost control of my movements. My heart pounded, I forgot about the shaking and drumming and felt my body rise up. There was a tremendous amount of nervous energy. At first, the shaking seemed to emanate from my genitals. I felt the drum rise up into the air, and the nervous feeling went along with it. The area near my solar plexus began to tremble, and then my chest, shoulders and finally my head. When I became conscious of these movements, fear swept through me. My mind split and I watched the body (me) shaking and jumping into the air, and I had no control over it.

Suddenly I found myself flying over a quiet valley towards a greenish glow. It was as though I were dreaming. A light appeared before me and consumed my attention. I saw a square structure like a three-story house whose bricks were meticulously laid. The doors and windows on the first two floors were closed; through the open windows in the top floor, I saw the upper torso of a green figure. I'm not certain what it was, but the green light emanated from what appeared to be an eye. I realized that I was dreaming, and felt water being poured on my head. In seconds, I was fully aware of my surroundings. Bhirendra smiled; he said I had been purified by the water sprinkled from a sacred bowl. It was time for the dawn march to the Śiva shrine.

Bhirendra analyzed my experience. He said the green form might have been the supernatural being possessing me. He considered this to be an unripe or "crude vision," unlike the controlled visions that appear to the shamans when they perform their duties and send their souls on journeys. He said he had visions like mine before he became fully initiated. Several of the other disciples also were "possessed" that night, and mumbled sounds that Bhirendra interpreted as words of spirits in the vicinity or, in one case, from the initiant's dead grandfather. None reported a vision. Later, Bhirendra explained that shamanic "clear" visions involve meeting the gods face to face in their golden palaces to receive powerful *mantra*. My vision was crazy because he did not recognize the form I described or the place I'd been.

We approached the Śiva shrine singing and drumming, and climbed the stairs that led to the rock representing Śiva. Many people stopped Bhirendra to ask about the "white" *bombo*. He explained that the gods came to me which impressed everyone and filled Bhirendra with pride. We played before the rock and all of the shamans shook simultaneously and were "possessed" by Śiva. I did not.

Relationship with the Guru

After Richeswar, the apprenticeship went downhill. Nothing could equal it. Several more purifications were held to entice the gods and dead relatives to possess me, but no experiences occurred to parallel the night at Richeswar. Bhirendra and I were disappointed. He wanted the god that shook (possessed) me to speak and identify itself. Then we could hold a *guru puja* (ritual) where the spirit would be honored and asked to become my tutelary deity. This now remains for future research.

In the remainder of time spent together, Bhirendra concentrated on detailing the shaman's belief system. This work after Richeswar was more in-depth than it had been before. So while my apprenticeship was only a limited success, the experiential technique was a success. Bhirendra revealed much of his system and explained the various stages involved in initiatory advancement. Some of this information might not have been attained by more traditional field methods, and I think Bhirendra revealed it primarily because of the guru-disciple relationship. I was taught as a student; he wanted me to understand everything in detail so that I could practice the teachings.

Our relationship remained unblemished until shortly before my departure. Bhirendra knew I respected and acknowledged his shamanic expertise. He considered me a serious student and respected my commitment. While I never became a Tamang, a level of human understanding was reached with my guru.

Just as our stay was drawing to a close, a series of crises befell my family. My son and I were bitten by a rabid dog, and a few days later my wife and I contracted hepatitis. I didn't call Bhirendra in to treat us; in fact I didn't even think of him then. I was frightened, and for a few days the possibility of death crossed my mind more than once. I sought out Western medical aid as quickly as possible. When Bhirendra learned of our problems, he came to my house, observably shaken. He asked me "not to tell anyone" that I hadn't called on him first, explaining he had told people that I had consulted him and that he had told me to go to a hospital. "What will the villagers think if they learn my disciple did not call me when illness struck? " I was speechless. At that moment, the gulf between us became apparent. There was great frustration between my desire to become a shaman and my inability to behave like one. I finally understood the limits of my participation. My method was a failure!

Shortly thereafter, I was hospitalized for the hepatitis. On the third night in the hospital, I dreamed I was running down the streets of Boudhanath pursued by a bull. I ran on top of a garbage heap. There was a stick in my hand and it was magically transformed into a bright yellow and black snake. I used it as a whip to chase the bull away. I cracked it over my head, and it sounded as loud as thunder; then I heard a voice reciting what seemed to be a *mantra* and turned to see Bhirendra. The dream was very vivid, with colors brighter than in waking life. I became aware that I was dreaming and began to awaken, still captivated by the dream images which carried over into ordinary reality. For a few moments, I could still see and hear Bhirendra.

The dream impressed me greatly; its images are still clear in my mind. It was one of those dreams, which Jung (1953:178; 1954:117-119; 1960:254; 1969a:293) called "big dreams," which appear at important junctures of life, often preceding personality change, sometimes even psychosis. Jung states that they are very numinous and carry a feeling of significance which is remembered for years but whose meaning is difficult to understand. During the days of my recovery, while I was laying in bed, the dream images often came to mind, preoccupying me.

Shortly after my release from the hospital, Bhirendra came to visit. I was compelled to tell him the dream, and as I began telling him, his eyes gleamed. He grew very excited and began interpreting the dream. He said that the voice I heard was his spirit, and his *mantra* had cured me. The bull was a spirit sent by a jealous shaman and was responsible for my misfortunes. His spirit had worked the magic that drove the bull away, and was the reason I was out of the hospital and feeling better. His emotional energy was contagious; my dream came alive. The dream images enveloped me and, as I relived them, I experienced a suspension of disbelief. It didn't occur to me then to question

Bhirendra's interpretation. Once the dream was interpreted, I felt an unmistakable "ah hah!" and thought: "The dream and illness are related. By chasing the bull away, I have been cured." The boundaries between dream and reality seemed to merge; what happened in the former had effects in the latter. My way of thinking was completely turned around. I stepped across cultural boundaries and was freed from my previous intellectual inflexibility. Emotion welled up inside me and I began to tremble and weep. Bhirendra and I embraced. In retrospect, this experience seems very close to what Maslow (1971:278) described as a "peak experience" in that it enabled me to transcend individual and cultural differences and attain a new viewpoint and feeling of oneness with another human being.

Bhirendra said my dream indicated I would have success becoming a shaman. He saw it as a sign of my calling. I was a "real" disciple now. He gave his magical dagger to me as a gift, to remind me of the pilgrimage and of how the gods had favored to possess me. He said that I would attain clear visions and we would fly together to the nine heavens. As I mentioned earlier, I am still skeptical that spirits exist, or that souls journey, and I have not experienced a conversion, but I do believe in the guru and in the effectiveness of the shamans' techniques.

My experience is similar to what a Tamang neophyte might experience with his guru. One of the primary things the guru does for his disciple is to interpret the calling and place it within a socio-cultural context so that it can be utilized. Bhirendra did this for me. He provided order in a chaotic situation, assuring me of recovery, and linking this with initiatory advancement. By recovering, I became a better disciple. Bhirendra treated my problem as though it were symptomatic of an "initiatory sickness," the beginning of a shamanic journey.

Now, whether I will actually become a Tamang shaman is questionable. As mentioned, I have not experienced cultural conversion. My purpose has remained to study altered states of consciousness and for this purpose I believe the experiential method is a viable and important aid. The guru-disciple relationship enhanced the quality and type of data I received. I was concerned with introspective states and because I attempted to experience them as an initiant, I came to appreciate their significance within the shamanic system. That is,while my own initiations were only partially successful, I experienced them in the same context as other Tamang shamans. "Crude visions" and the shaking characteristic of spirit possession was experienced first-hand. The guru took notice of these psychological phenomena and, by way of explanation attempted to make me aware of initiatory goals. Of course, my apprenticeship has only begun but, in a real sense, the information contained herein was learned as an "insider" in spite of the fact that I am not a Tamang.

CHAPTER FOUR

Tamang Religious Specialists

Tamang religion is essentially comprised of two distinct yet coexisting systems, Buddhism and shamanism. These are the traditionally recognized aspects. Hinduism, which will be discussed in relation to Tamang religion in Chapter 5, has also had a great influence. However, the Tamang do not consider themselves Hindu and none of their religious specialists espouse Hinduism.

The two major types of Tamang religious specialists are *lama* (priests) and *bombo* (shamans). Both are exclusively male professions. Tamang women sometimes enter the clergy by becoming nuns in Tibetan monasteries; there is no monastic life in Tamang Lamaism.

Lama and *bombo* fulfill different social functions in the community. As mentioned earlier, the *lama*'s primary responsibility is officiation at funeral ceremonies. The *bombo*'s main duty is to perform healing rituals. There is a Tamang myth that explains the separate and cooperative social functions of the two specialists whose belief systems are, in some ways, ideologically opposed to each other. The myth relates that:

> At one time, the *bombo* had all the religious responsibilities. They cured the sick and conducted souls to heaven during the funeral ceremony. However, the souls of the deceased were not reaching heaven so Guru Rinpoche (Padma Sambhava) decided to investigate. He went to a village where Nara Bon Chen (the first human shaman) was conducting a funeral service. Nara played the drum

9. Tamang lamas performing a *ghe-wa* (funeral ceremony) by reading and chanting from the Tibetan Book of the Dead, accompanying themselves on their horns and percussions. The trays of food and incense offerings are for the gods and spirits depicted by elaborate dough effigies. The Buddhas, in their various incarnations, are depicted on the sacred painted scrolls.

and called on the deceased's spirit to enter a wooden effigy dressed in the dead man's clothes. The effigy began to shake (indicating that the soul had entered it) and Nara questioned it about the causes of death, afterworld existence, etc. The effigy responded by nodding yes or no. Disguised as a beggar, Guru Rinpoche watched the proceedings and then flashed his *dorje*[1] at the effigy, causing it to fall to the ground. Nara tried in vain to animate the effigy but the ceremony came to an abrupt halt. Nara went through the village looking for the cause of the problem. He was told that a stranger, dressed as a beggar, had come into the village and quickly departed, saying: "Your souls are not reaching heaven because Nara takes life making sacrifices. Henceforth the *lama* will lead them." Nara chased after Guru Rinpoche and, when he found him, challenged him to a race to the top of a mountain with the winner to assume all the religious responsibilities. The race began. Nara played the drum and was thereby propelled up the mountain. Guru Rinpoche changed himself into a vulture and caught up with Nara just below the mountain peak, tripping him and causing him to fall into a bed of nettles. Enraged, Nara said a *mantra* causing a swarm of bees to attack Guru Rinpoche. They stung his face and neck but Guru Rinpoche was bound as a Buddhist not to harm them. Standing at the top of the mountain, he offered Nara a compromise: "Send away the bees and retain some of your powers." So Nara dispatched the bees and healed Guru Rinpoche's wounds, whereupon it was decided that Nara would retain his healing abilities. Thus, among the Tamang, the *bombo* still cure the sick.

[1] *Dorje* is the Tibetan equivalent of the Sanskrit *vajra*, or thunderbolt. *Do* means "stone," *rje* "ruler." The *dorje*, therefore is king of stones, the most precious and powerful of all stones, the diamond. Although different in function and meaning, the *dorje* could be compared in importance to the Christian cross (see Govinda 1960:61f for its sacred Tibetan Buddhist meaning).

This interesting myth is of Tamang origin, but similar myths occur among the Tibetan Kargyüdpa *lama* sect. In the latter tale, the battle takes place between Milarepa and Nara Bon at Kailāsa, a holy mountain in western Tibet. My Tamang informants placed the battle at Ganesh Himal where Nepal's Rasua district borders on Tibet.[2] In the 11th century Kargyüdpa version, Milarepa defeated Nara outright; no bee episode is mentioned. In yet another version, this one from the "white" (written as opposed to oral) Bon religion, Nara is the clear-cut winner (Hoffman 1961:25,99). The compromise occurring in the Tamang myth reflects the accommodation and coexistence of the two distinct religions in Tamang society.

Bonpoism can be divided into three stages (Li An-Che 1948: 33-36). The first is that of primitive Bon, otherwise known as "the black sect." The second phase ended during the reign of the mythical King Gri-gumTsan-po. The third phase began during the reign of Srong Tsen Gampo (620-649 A.D.), the first Buddhist king of Tibet. It was during this third phase that the textual white Bon achieved full development. Black and white Bon are completely different religions. The former is a form of shamanism and animism with an oral tradition. White Bon is close to Buddhism, assimilating almost all its literature. Li An-Che (1948: 31) writes, "The names of deities and scriptures in (white) Bonism are different from those in Lamaism but their functions and ideologies correspond." (parenthesis mine).

Tamang Bomboism is probably very close to ancient black Bon. Both are shamanic-type religions with oral traditions. And none of the Tamang *bombo* interviewed knew of white Bon or its deities.[3] Further, and most particularly, Bomboism is an

[2] T. Hagan (1961:66-67) writes that the Tamang's "... original Nepalese home is on the southern flank of Ganesh Himal, bounded on the east by the Tirsuli River and on the west by the Buri Gandaki."

[3] Because of the absence of these deities and of Srong Tsen Gampo from the Tamang oral tradition, it seems likely that the Tamang either left Tibet before his reign; or have always lived where they do now, between Kathmandu and Tibet where the Himalayan Mountains provided a natural barrier against early incursion of Buddhism or white Bon philosophy.

ecstatic religion in which the specialist enters into trance; i.e., he becomes possessed by spirits and embarks on soul journeys. The ritualistic duties of the *lama*, on the other hand, are textual and non-inspirational. There is no direct encounter with the supernatural. Tamang say "the lama proceeds step by step" (according to a prescribed litany), "the *bombo* by his voice" (inspired by the gods and spirits that possess him during the ritual) (cf. Höfer 1974:172).

A key distinction between *bombo* and *lama* occurs regarding the morality of sacrifice. The *lama* believe that the punishment for taking life is eternal torment in hell. But the shamans consider sacrifice to be an integral part in the performance of their duties. Bhirendra explained by saying, "The spirits are hungry; if they are not fed they will eat the people." When evil spirits attack, they are believed to cause illness by consuming their victims. To combat such illnesses, the shaman often makes sacrifice to these spirits; that is, he feeds them.

The shamans feel that they are rewarded for performing this task by earning merit and *karma* for a better rebirth. And, while the *lama* consider sacrifice to be a sin, they hire others to make sacrifices for them. One Tin Chuli *lama* who thought that the gods had granted him a favor hired Bhirendra to make the sacrifice he had promised them. When questioned regarding the gap between the real and the ideal, he countered saying he was not cutting the animal himself.

Lamaism may not have entered Tamang religion until the 11th or 12th century, since there is a Tamang myth that explains that the six *lama* clans (see Chapter 3, note 13) are descended from Lhalung Paidorje, the monk who actually killed the evil king Lang Dharma. At that time, there was strife between competing sects and monasteries in Tibet, and some monks were forced to flee to Nepal. Before the reign of the 1st Dalai Lama, Ge-Dun-Dub (1431-1475), leadership within monasteries was hereditarily passed from father to son, or from paternal uncle to nephew in the celibate sects (see Stein 1972:106). So, it is possible that groups of emigrating monks were accepted into Tamang society as clans.

There are also similarities between *lama* and *bombo* philosophy. The *lama* appeal to various different Buddhas, all of whom are subservient to the One from which everything derives, the Adi-Buddha. Similarly, the *bombo* main god, Ghesar Gyalpo,[4] commands the other gods and spirits, and is often equated with the Adi-Buddha by the shamans. Also, the Indian concept of *karma* is accepted by both religions and generally acknowledged by the lay population. Since they are not mutually exclusive, the *lama* employ *bombo* and vice versa. The people tolerate the obvious contradictions by saying that "everything is one" at bottom.

Shaman as Sorcerer

There is a myth that explains why the *bombo* tradition is maintained orally. It tells of yet another disagreement between Guru Rinpoche and Nara Bon:

> One day Guru Rinpoche set out to fool Nara and cause him to lose some of his powers. So he bragged that he had burned all his books because he knew everything and no longer needed them. Not wanting to be shown up, Nara threw his books into a fire. When they were aflame, Guru Rinpoche reached into his jacket to reveal his texts, and laughed at Nara for being so stupid. Nara reached into the fire and ate all the ashes, saying "I am as powerful as you, but I do not need texts for I have committed everything to memory."

Thus the *bombo* commit everything to memory. Each of my informants could recite hundreds of *mantra* and *sherab*, word for word.

Even though this well-known myth shows how the *lama*

[4]The *bombo* deny any knowledge of Ghesar of Ling (David-Neel 1959), a mythical Tibetan cultural hero with shamanic origins (Stein 1972:223), nor does there appear to be any thematic similarity between him and Ghesar Gyalpo, the Tamang "High God," ruler and judge of the universe.

tricked the *bombo*, in everyday life it is the shaman whose honesty is questioned. The people extol the *lama*'s virtue and decry the *bombo*'s guile. *Bombo* tell stories of how "other" shamans used their magical formulae to gain control over evil spirits for their own benefit. The villagers both fear their power and need their help to keep the spirits at bay. The shamans' power can be used as they desire; it is neutral. Consequently, the *lama* are entrusted with all the political offices in the villages.

So the *bombo* is a sorcerer[5] capable of good or evil. He will confront the spirits on his patient's behalf in long, dramatic healing rituals. Or he can command the spirits to deliver harm. Bhirendra said he was sometimes approached by individuals who wanted him to send "magic arrows" against a foe. There was ostensibly some good cause (like revenge), and Bhirendra complied if he felt such action was deserved.[6] He confided that he had sent arrows against his ex-wife and a *lama* who had conspired to cheat him out of his property. There are numerous ways in which the *bombo* can inflict harm. Our housekeeper was in a state of perpetual anxiety because of the shamans who routinely came to visit, and she kept me alerted to potential dangers. She would not allow us to eat in front of the *bombo* (they could blow a *mantra* onto our food), and was very disturbed about the countless cups of tea we all drank together.

My shaman informants were like the classic trickster figure with that same ambivalence of character noticed by Radin (1956: xxiii): "The trickster is at one and the same time creator and destroyer, giver and negator, he who dupes others and is always duped himself." I asked Bhirendra if he lived up to the shaman's scandalous reputation. He answered by way of analogy, saying

[5] The Tamang do not recognize the same distinction between sorcery and witchcraft as the Azande (Evans-Pritchard 1976). They do not acknowledge unconscious witchcraft. Every act of a shaman or witch is conscious and involves definite ritual procedures.

[6] Similar to the Tenino shamans of the Pacific Northwest (Murdock 1965:170), the Tamang *bombo* use their powers of sorcery for judicial purposes.

"When you stick your finger into a bowl of *ghiu* (clarified butter), a lot more will cling to the finger if it is crooked than if it is straight."

Types of Bombo

There are a number of different types of *bombo*. Munsor and Dunsor Bons are those who work at night and in the day respectively. Dunsor Bons previously performed the funeral ceremonies (always conducted during the day), but, as related in detail above, have lost that responsibility. They officiate at clan rituals, celebrated annually at different times by different clans. A virgin sheep is generally sacrificed at these events. The *bombo* performing the *puja* must be of the same clan as those celebrating it. Munsor Bons conduct healing rituals, which are always held at night. Bhirendra was both a Munsor and Dunsor Bon.

The Rhan Sing Tungba Bon is a "self-created" *bombo*, so called because he becomes a shaman from personal necessity and not from choice. The Rhan Sing Tungba experiences a "calling" which is an initial affliction whose only cure is to shamanize. In a typical calling, the Rhan Sing Tungba loses control of his behavior, says crazy things, and shakes from head to toe. Thus afflicted, he wanders into the forest alone in a semi-conscious state, seeking solitude (see Chapter 6). Bhirendra, who is a Rhan Sing Tungba, says a man who refuses the call will surely die. After the initial calling, the Rhan Sing Tungba will find a shaman guru from whom to learn methods and techniques of ritual, as do the other types of shamans. However, not all shamans experience an initiatory calling: choosing to become shamans for reasons of profit, power, human kindness, etc.

There are also categories for white and black *bombo*. Black *bombo* are those who "play" with evil spirits, using them as "secret weapons" to be dispatched at will to harm or even kill. Black *bombo* keep these malevolent beings under control by feeding them (i.e., sacrificing food to them). If they become hungry, they can turn on the *bombo* and his family members. Villagers employ shamans to use these spirits to protect their fields, guard their homes when they are away, and the like. In other words, there is social value to the black arts.

White *bombo* call on and use the power of the gods for curing and other community benefit, and to outsmart and battle the evil spirits, some of which have been sent by black shamans and witches. Many shaman perform both black and white functions. Bhirendra explained that a shaman who is only black is no better than a witch; neither do any good. Conversely, a shaman who is only white limits the scope of his power; Bhirendra likened a white shaman to a man who cannot make up his mind whether to become a shaman or a *lama*. Yet, while these categories are distinguished from each other, I never met a shaman who claimed to be exclusively black or white. Bhirendra admitted to playing with spirits, but never for evil purposes.

10. The main shrine at the Boudha *stupa* belongs to Ajima, Hindu goddess of disease.

CHAPTER FIVE

Indigenous Medical Systems

Spirits in Nepalese Religion and Medicine

The Tamang believe that spirits are a principle part of the organization and meaning of the mundane world. They participate in the ordinary world, affecting the lives of men for good and evil. Further, they are the means by which the Tamang articulate to themselves the reasons for misfortune. The Tamang medical system revolves around spirits as they relate to illness and misfortune.

Tamang consider themselves Buddhist, as opposed to Hindu, but the distinction is not absolute in Nepal. Tamang celebrate every important and many lesser Hindu holidays, along with the vast majority of the other people who live in the Valley. They have adopted many Hindu customs: many of the men shave their heads when their father dies, and wear all-white clothing for the year following. They consult Hindu Brahman-astrologers. Perhaps 80% of the gods and spirits worshipped by the Tamang are Hindu in name (see Höfer 1969:78).

This blending of religious practices and faiths pervades the Valley. Gujeswari, the Hindu mother-goddess, is taken to be the *śakti* (female aspect) of the Adi-Buddha by the Buddhists, and that of Śiva by the Hindus. Daksin Kali, a Tantric Buddhist goddess, is feasted with sacrifices offered by Hindus and Buddhists alike every Tuesday and Saturday (see Hasrat 1970:xx,7,12-13). In any other country, Buddhists would not be making sacrifices. At Swayambu, where the Adi-Buddha first appeared in Nepal, there is a temple for the Hindu grandmother goddess of disease, Ajima. As mentioned earlier, Ajima is also the main goddess of the *stupa* at Boudha, where her shrine is maintained by the Chinea Lama and his disciples. And, at many of the Newari Buddhist monasteries in the Valley, Buddhist *dorje* (diamond scepters) and Śiva *linga* (phalluses) are next to each other.

This admixture appears in Nepal's earliest Hindu and Buddhist literature. The *Vamśavali* texts of both faiths contain many borrowings and references to each other's deities (Hasrat 1970: xxf). The blending of rituals and beliefs is the most salient feature of the syncretic Nepalese religions.

Tamang shamanism has incorporated many deities and tales from Hinduism and Buddhism and woven them into a unique tradition. The *sherab* myths feature Hindu and Buddhist characters in dominant roles. This mixing of traditions is also reflected in the language used in the Tamang oral texts. Some myths are partly related in Old Tamang (similar to classical Tibetan), partly in Tamang, and partly in Nepali.

But shamanism is not just another element to be listed alongside Buddhism and Hinduism. As noted by Jones (1968:311), analyzing shamanism in South Asia as just another category distorts native views. He writes, "Shamanism does not exist . . . as a 'complementary' religious rite to Hinduism, nor . . . to Buddhism . . . but is part and parcel of these great religions as a whole."

Shamanism is the unwritten religion of the Tamang. It is an animistic religion that postulates numerous categories of spirit beings. Throughout Nepal, among all the various groups, whether of Aryan or Tibetan extraction, there is an underlying belief in spirit beings. When a Nepalese is ill, he is likely to turn first to a shaman, the religious specialist who can effectively deal with the spirits.

The Tamang animistic-shamanic belief system has never been overcome by Hinduism or Buddhism; it is not mere survival but the dynamic synthesizing force of Tamang religion. The great majority of Tamang know nothing about Buddhist dogma and sects. Even many of the *lama* know little about the sacred scriptures and spend little time in meditation. Neither is there much knowledge of the complex mythology and philosophy surrounding their Hindu deities. But everyone was well acquainted with the spirits and knew all the names of those that lived in places in and around their village. The people know which spirit lives in trees, rocks, at crossroads; they know who each spirit was before death and how it came to inhabit its place. Further, it is often to placate these spirits, to alleviate the suffering they cause, that a Tamang goes to the various Buddhist and Hindu shrines.

Although the conclusions drawn here are based on work with the Tamang, interviews with Newari, Tibetan, Magar and other tribal group members, Brahmans and Chetris seem to suggest that animism is the fiber holding Buddhism and Hinduism together in the unique blend characterizing Nepalese religion in the Kathmandu Valley.

The concepts of "great tradition" and "little tradition" are not applicable in Nepal (Redfield 1955). Tamang religion is not the result of a sophisticated urban religion imposing itself onto a folk society. Like most of the Tibeto-Burmese speaking groups that comprise the majority of Nepal's population, the Tamang claim to be Buddhist and, as discussed in the previous chapter, received Buddhism and its literature indirectly from Tibet. Further, the ruling Hindus who conquered and unified Nepal came from Gorkha in central Nepal, which is not a complex urban society. The Tamang assimilated various aspects of both religions and their literature. The forge upon which this was accomplished was the animistic belief system. The belief in spirits is all-pervasive in Nepal; it dominates life in city and country alike, in Boudha, Tin Chuli and Kathmandu city (see Okaha 1976).

Animism is not the same in all its particulars among all Nepalese people. But there is enough commonality and flexibility in the belief systems of the different ethnic groups to allow for easy communication about these issues between individuals from various different groups. For example, ethnically distinct shamans are frequently called in to perform healing rituals for different groups. I have witnessed Tamang healing Chetri, Sherpa healing Tamang, and similar examples by Tibetan and Newari healers. This is not in the least unorthodox; shamans of any ethnic group may take members of another group as disciples. Bhirendra had five disciples: one Newar, one Chetri, one American, and two Tamang. Another Tamang informant had a Gurung guru. Macdonald (1976a:310) writes of the shaman: "He can . . . be of any *jat*,[1] and take as a pupil a person of any other caste."

Again, this does not imply that there is only one animistic system in Nepal; only that most Nepalese are more aware of the similarities between their beliefs than their differences, and are therefore able to understand and participate in one another's rituals. Macdonald (1975b:113f) demonstrated that the shaman is a pan-Nepali phenomenon; my position is that the universe in which the shaman participates is, in many essentials, pan-Nepali.

Traditional Categories of Illness

For the Tamang, the world of spirits cannot be radically separated from the mundane world. Illnesses and other troubles that disrupt the normal flow of existence are attributed to the many spirits inhabiting the world. In the process of diagnosis, the shaman resorts to these explanatory devices to articulate and explain the cause of physical and mental disease, and household problems.

Central to Tamang concepts of illness are categories of gods, spirits and witches. Included in the god category are nine planets (*graha*). *Graha* are not planets in the conventional sense. They are not elliptical bodies traveling in orbit through the universe; one is described as a shoemaker, others have animal form. But all cause one to be unlucky during one's "bad days." Bad days are determined by age with even years unlucky, odd years fortunate. One is susceptible to misfortune only during bad days.

The way the shamans explained this confusing system of planets brought the complex Hindu astrology to mind. However,

[1] The term *jat* applies not only to occupational groupings but also to designate ethnic groups. Turner (1931:213) defines it as "sort, kind, tribe, nation, or caste."

the Tamang have no such astrological setup. When a Tamang needs to know about his good days, e.g., in order to plan a wedding, etc., a Brahman is consulted.

Bhirendra explained that the *graha* bring bad luck, making a person vulnerable to attack by witches or spirits that cause illness. At most healing rituals, and rituals dealing with other types of misfortune, the shaman makes an offering of food and incense to the *graha*.

Also in the category of gods are the *khorwa lha* (Ta.), literally "gods of the atmosphere and earth." Included in this group are those who protect villages (like Ajima at Boudha), and those who live in the four directions. These gods have local shrines in and around villages and their influence is usually limited to these localities. One notable exception is Samsari Devi (goddess of the world); she moves freely in the atmosphere, having no specific shrine or location, and is the goddess believed to cause epidemic disease. Any of the *khorwa* deities can cause illness to individuals who encroach upon their territory irresponsibly, who disturb their shrine, or who fail to perform proper homage. The *khorwa* deities do not attack unprovoked.

Khorwa deities are different from evil spirits (*lagu*). While the *khorwa* spirits can strike out and cause illness, they can also protect and bestow favors when worshipped regularly. *Lagu*, on the other hand, are totally evil. They come in different varieites but all have one thing in common: they are the disenchanted souls of people who have died in unnatural ways, e.g., by accident, suicide, murder or execution. A dead man's soul may also become a *lagu* if he has not received a proper funeral.

Some of the various kinds of *lagu* are called *bayu*, *bhut*, *pret*, *pichas*, *masaan*, *nag* and *moch*. There is little agreement as to how each of these different types came into existence. Yet each possesses certain characteristics distinguishing it from the others. For example, a *masaan* looks like a skeleton and hangs around graveyards. *Nag* take the form of serpents. *Moch* attack children. Some say that *bayu* cause heart pain, and *nag* eye trouble; but aside from these two, the different kinds of *lagu* do not cause unique symptoms. Just as Western laymen rely on doctors to diagnose the causes of illness, so Tamang laymen leave it to the *bombo.* However, the *bombo* do not agree about which spirit causes which illness.

Spirit-caused illnesses are divided by the Tamang into four categories: attack, bewitchment, loss of soul, and spirit possession. The verb *lagnu* (to attack) is used to describe the onslaught of the *lagu* spirits, and all these spirits, as mentioned before, attack because they are hungry, and are appeased and dispatched by food offerings made by the shaman. Stone's (1976:58) analysis of *lagu* in a Brahman-Chetri village in Newakot district applies equally to the Tamang in Boudha/Tin Chuli. She writes:

> Despite their descriptive differences, all of these spirits share in common the ability to harm people or their livestock through causing illness or death. Further all attack from hunger; and their attack is designed to elicit food offerings from their victims. Sometimes these offerings are considered as a substitute for the victim's own body which the spirit desires to eat. Finally, all these spirits attack of their own volition or at the direction of a *bokshi* (witch). (parenthesis mine).

It is believed that witches gain control over *lagu* by promising them food. Witches do not always use spirits to cause illness, however. They are said to have techniques known in the literature as contagious and sympathetic magic. A witch may collect things belonging to the victim (pieces of fingernails, hair, clothing, etc.), or draw an effigy, and work harm on these objects to cause similar misfortune to befall the victim.

Bokshi are believed to be real people but, to my knowledge, their identity is never divulged. When the shaman diagnoses attack by a *bokshi* as the cause of his patient's illness, using techniques that will be discussed in detail later, he attempts to determine who the *bokshi* is. In every case I witnessed, the attempt was unsuccessful. Often there were hints; allegations were made that an old woman from a village a few miles distant was causing harm, but identity was never determined. Sometimes the witch's clan or village was mentioned, but nothing more specific was revealed.

Witchcraft accusation might have been more precise among Tamang living in the Valley years ago. In fact, there are Tamang villages west of the Valley where witchcraft accusations are said to be specific and may in fact reflect social conflicts[2] (cf. Evans-Pritchard 1976). This also seems to be the case among some groups of Chetri in central Nepal (Blustain 1976). But a statute enacted by Jung Bahadur Rana in 1853, making false accusation of witchcraft a punishable crime, is enforced in the Valley. Conviction of this crime is punishable by a fine of 60 rupees, a large sum for an average Nepalese (see Macdonald 1976b).

The third category whereby spirits cause illness is through soul loss. Fright is the only way one can lose a soul. When frightened, a person's soul leaves his body through the top of his head. When this happens, it can be stolen by any of the *lagu*. A person suffering from soul loss is depressed, becomes forgetful, weak; he loses weight and, in extreme cases, wanders around in a fugue state, sometimes near places thought to be impure (*jutho*) like cemeteries. I observed only one case of soul loss and it was complicated by ailments attributed to other categories as well.

Possession is the opposite of soul loss. It is an intrusion (or gain), rather than the loss of a soul. A possessed person manifests antisocial behavior. He does things as though he were another person: argues with his family, says irrational things, has temper tantrums, and is at moments beset with anxiety. During possession-trances occurring in rituals, patients may tremble all over, sometimes writhing on the ground or crying out obscenities. Shaking is the key symptom of possession-trance. Possession experiences are followed by amnesia. The Tamang clearly differentiate between the patient's pathological spirit possession and soul loss, and the shaman's non-pathological possession-trance and magical flight which are voluntary, occur only in ritual performances, and are remembered.

In Tamang society, a person who is involuntarily possessed is

[2] Personal conversation with David Holmberg. Holmberg conducted anthropological research with Tamang residing in the Bagmati Zone west of Kathmandu.

11. **A shaman makes** his in tial diagnosis by feeling his patient's pulse.

believed to be the victim of a spirit. The intruding spirit sometimes causes the patient to speak, sometimes not. But it always causes trembling. In rituals, the trembling builds to a crescendo before the epileptoid seizure ends (see Chapter 7).

Shamanism and Medicine

Aside from spirit-caused illnesses, there are natural illnesses. They may be mild, like a stomach ache caused by eating something wrong, or a cold resulting from bad weather. In cases of natural illness, Bhirendra recommends bed rest or change in diet. He does not perform *puja* for patients suffering from natural causes.

For the more severe forms of natural illness, Bhirednra recommends that the patient seek modern medical aid. However, there are no precise boundaries between natural and spirit-caused illnesses. The diagnostic decisions appear to be based on experience; Bhirendra intuitively knew what he could treat successfully, and what he could not. He frequently acknowledged that doctors are superior at treating cholera and preventing rabies, and at treating severe lacerations and the like. Patients who were almost totally incapacitated by their illnesses were generally those referred to doctors. There was an old man who lived around the *stupa* whose illness had relegated him to bed for several months. He manifested symptoms like those of emphysema. The man was certain that a witch had put something into his food and poisoned him. Bhirendra was called in, and he diagnosed that this was not the case. There were no witches or *lagu* involved in the old man's sickness. He suggested that he go to the hospital. The man replied that the doctors at the hospital had been unable to help him, and insisted that Bhirendra perform a healing *puja*. That night, Bhirendra failed to show up at the appointed time. The old man sent people to find him, but Bhirendra feigned illness and refused to leave his house. He told me later that he was certain the old man was dying, and it created a problem for him. It would be a bad thing to tell the old man he was going to die. But, if he performed the *puja* and then the fellow died, people would "lose confidence" in his powers. So Bhirendra completely avoided any involvement. The patient died a few weeks later.

Bhirendra's father also suffered from a respiratory problem. There were times that the old gentleman was completely debilitated. Still, Bhirendra did no *puja* for him. Rather he brought him down to the hospital occasionally. There were other cases where Bhirendra performed a ritual that failed to evoke a positive result. In these cases, too, he suggested modern medical assistance.

Gould (1957:508f) sets forth a division of role resposibility between doctor and folk healer in northern India that, in some respects, applies to the Tamang. According to him, the traditional healers consider critically disabling illnesses to be the province of the doctors; illnesses that allow the sufferer to maintain a semblance of his daily routine are the realm of the shaman. The four categories of spirit illness detailed above (attack, bewitchment, soul loss, possession) are all of this latter type. Tamang shamans also recommend medical treatment for chronic and progressing disorders like the cases above. Bhirendra's greatest success is with illnesses that are sudden in onset, yet not incapacitating.

It is also interesting to mention that this same distinction applies to "psychiatric" diagnoses. Chronic psychopathic syndromes, which include symptoms often associated with psychosis like delusions of grandeur, persecutory delusions, depressions and "uninfluenceability" (lack of transference?), are considered "crazy" (*bowla*) and untreatable by shamans. *Bowla* is contrasted to *lagu* illnesses that are thought to be sudden in onset and less functionally incapacitating. This indigenous Tamang classification seems similar to the modern concepts distinguishing between psychosis and neurosis. The shamans see themselves as effective only with the latter.

The distinction the Tamang make between natural and spirit caused illnesses corresponds to Foster's (1978) categories of "personalistic" and "naturalistic" types of disease etiology and medical systems. The latter describes modern medicine which explains illness as due to natural causes; the former is the "primitive" medical systems that typically employ personalistic causes (witches and spirits) to illness. As is obvious from the Tamang medical beliefs, the two systems are not mutually exclusive, coexisting in the same culture, representing health care options to be exploited for different reasons.

Generally, the Tamang recognize that medicine cures symptoms but that many diseases are caused by spirit agents for which a shaman is required. While they have seen certain advantages result from modern medical treatment, they by no means understand or completely accept it. They pragmatically avail themselves of its technology, but this causes no damage to their basic folk ideology. For example, if a patient visits the doctor after the shaman's ritual fails to provide relief from the ailment, the shaman will still take credit for the successful resolution of the problem. After all, his ritual did away with the spirits that are the primary cause of the illness. The doctor merely speeded along relief of the symptoms, which would have occurred eventually anyway. Thus modern medicine is filtered through an indigenous cultural screen and has therefore not done violence to the role of the Tamang shaman (cf. Gould 1957).

Nor has the shaman's function inhibited the penetration of modern medicine. The shaman is an astute observer of his community. His fellow villagers not only come to him when they are ill but interact with him on a day-to-day basis. He soon knows if his rituals are successful, and there is nothing in his belief system to prevent him from suggesting that his patients seek medical treatment. Thus shamanism is not a critical block to medical treatment where serious illness is involved. The Tamang shaman has implicitly attuned his system to take advantage of medicine.

In fact, with proper training, the shamans can help spread medical aid inasmuch as they already recognize their own limitations in the treatment of certain illnesses and urge their patients to avail themselves of such treatment. In order to ease cultural transition, modern medicine must respect the shaman's positive role since both share a common goal: the alleviation of suffering, albeit each approaches this goal in a different, but not exclusive, way.

Landy (1974:103f) describes the adaptive curing role of the

shaman who is able to bridge the gap and borrow from scientific medicine while maintaining an effective relationship with his community. Here the shaman is a "cultural broker" and a valuable resource in situations of cultural change. In several developing areas, psychiatrists and other medical health professionals have established cooperative relationships with native healers, and these have enhanced health care (see Carstairs and Kapur 1976; Jelek 1974; Lambo 1964).

It is my belief that a cooperative relationship with the shaman can make the introduction and maintenance of Western health care less contradictory to traditional values. Since the shaman is in daily contact with his fellows, he could well be in collaboration with physicians and psychiatrists for the community good. Each specialist could maintain his own assumptive world, provide treatment within his own sphere of action, and transfer or triage mutual clients, supplementing rather than rivaling one another. Such interchange, necessary for the acceptance and establishment of scientific medicine, depends on the ability of medical specialists to become familiar with the socio-cultural conditions and beliefs of the people (see Foster 1976; Paul 1955).[3]

[3] It should be noted that HMG's Ministry of Health explicitly recognizes the value of traditional healers, has plans to incorporate them into the integrated health service projects, and in no way intends for modern medicine to replace them outright (Dr. L. Stone: personal communication).

CHAPTER SIX

The Shaman's Trance: Initiation and Psychotherapy

Shamanic Transmission and Psychopathology

The process of becoming a Tamang shaman is a long and arduous one. The training is both transic and didactic. It involves mastering a trance state which, at first, overwhelms the individual and makes him mad; there are also numerous *mantra* and myths to be memorized. In order to become a shaman, one must be very dedicated. Years of effort are required (Bhirendra served a 7-year apprenticeship); and when completed, the financial rewards are inconsequential. Yet there are individuals who want to be shamans. Three of Bhirendra's disciples came to the profession voluntarily for personal reasons. The other two disciples had to become shamans because they experienced an involuntary "calling," indigenously interpreted to be an affliction, as had Bhirendra when he was 13-years old. This chapter discusses the psychological aspects of the calling and other trance states experienced by the shaman during apprenticeship.

The unsolicited altered state of consciousness afflicting future shamans is called "crazy possession" (Ta: *lha khoiba mayba*). In this mental state, the neophyte shakes convulsively, indicating that he is possessed but not knowing why or by what. At times, he may shout incoherently or weep. He may see visions, but they are unstructured and chaotic. As mentioned earlier, Bhirendra called these "crude visions." The future *bombo*'s family becomes concerned because the young man forgets to eat and becomes weak. Eventually he may run into the forest naked and live with the animals for several days.

12. A shaman possessed by spirits.

While the calling is involuntary and spontaneous, it is also similar to what Krader (1967:114) terms "quasi-hereditary" in that transmission of shamanic powers occurs within a lineage but not to a predetermined individual. The Tamang believes that dead shamans normally choose the male patrilineal kinsman they prefer.

When Bhirendra was 13, he was stricken with *lha khoiba mayba*. The spirit that possessed him was his dead patrilineal grandfather, who chose Bhirendra over his brothers and other male kin. According to the Tamang, the power (*śakti*) of the dead *bombo* searches for a "religious person," one who can carry on his duties. The possessing spirit eventually becomes the young shaman's tutelary spirit (*mukhiya guru*).

Transmission of shamanic power may occur in a number of ways, sometimes at a deceased *bombo*'s funeral. Bhirendra told me about the ritual which purifies a dead *bombo*. It is performed before the funeral ceremony conducted by the *lama*, if the latter is to be done at all. In the ritual, all of the deceased *bombo*'s paraphernalia is placed on a platform. Family members and close friends sit around it, and an officiating shaman plays the drum and asks the spirit of the dead *bombo* to rest on the platform. The spirit is entreated not to be angry or cause trouble to his family, and invited to become a household deity. The spirit is also asked not to take his *śakti* and *mantra* out of the world with him, but to transmit them to one of the living. Later in the ritual, a son or grandson may begin to shake, indicating that he is the one chosen. The possession may be controlled or uncontrolled depending on whether the individual has had previous initiatory experience, and on the extent of that experience. The dead *bombo*'s spirit may again possess the person and, if he has not hitherto embarked upon the shaman's vocation, the spirit is likely to make him mad, inflicting him with the calling. In any case, the spirit will eventually reveal *mantra* and impart power, appearing to the chosen person in dreams and visions. This person inherits the deceased's ritual gear: drum, magical dagger, rosaries, and bells bound on belts designed to be worn over the shoulders.

When the shamanic vocation is transmitted through a spontaneous calling, it is very similar to what Czaplicka (1914:178), in a discussion of Siberian shamanism, describes as a "hereditary disease" in which the office of shaman remains within a family yet makes the new possessor suffer greatly. The following narrative is Bhirendra's description of his initiatory calling:

> When I was 13, I became possessed. I later learned that the spirit was my dead grandfather who had disappeared on a salt-trading mission to Tibet nine years earlier. At this time, I did not know what was happening to me. I would start shaking violently and be unable to sit still even for a minute, even at times that I was not trembling. My grandfather made me mad through possession, and I ran off into the forest, naked, for three days. During these three days, I ate only what was given me by my grandfather and the other spirits known as forest shamans, who wore pointed hats over their white hair and were only three feet tall. Their wives had black hair, long breasts and were very fat. When one came to get me, my grandfather stood in front to protect me from the frightening creature. One of the forest shamans wanted to teach me and gave me *sakti*. One of them gave me a *mantra* and fed me earthworms. You have to eat what they give you or you will die. Still, each time I reached for the worms, one of the females whipped my hands. She carried a gold sword and, each time she whipped me, she yelled "Let's cut off his head!" But the forest shaman said "No," because he wanted to teach me. Then he told me the correct way to take the food was with the back of my hands. When I did this, I was not attacked.
>
> Finally, all the people in the village came looking for me. They shoulted out my name throughout the forest. But instead of hearing voices, I heard dogs barking and ran away. Finally the villagers caught up with me and I stopped shivering and woke up. I was taken to the village and offered food. My family was very concerned; I had no appetite and that night began shaking again. This time, I took my father's (also a shaman) drum and went to where the three rivers cross (a cemetery). The villagers did not follow me, for the gods had opened up a path. Even if someone had followed me, they would not have seen the

> path I was taking. They would walk into trees and thorns, and fall off cliffs. In the cemetery, I saw many *lagu*, some with long crooked fangs, others with no heads and eyes in the middle of their chests, still others carrying death flags and decaying corpses. They chased me. Before I knew it, they were on top of me and devouring my body. I was horribly afraid and, in a last hope, cried out for the gods to save me, telling them I was only a young boy. I drew out my father's magical dagger to defend myself, but it fell to the ground and struck a rock. This created a spark of light and everything changed. Suddenly it was daytime and the demons were gone. I was alive! (Parenthesis mine.)

When Bhirendra returned home, he related his vision to his parents. Although his father was a *bombo*, it was decided that his maternal uncle, a very powerful shaman, would become the boy's guru. He taught Bhirendra all the ritual methods and *mantra* he knew. And, from the time his training began, Bhirendra's grandfather was his "internal guru," visiting him in his dreams to give him special instructions and *mantra*. That is, his dead grandfather's spirit, which had initially possessed Bhirendra and made him mad, became his chief tutelary spirit (*mukhiya guru*). Whenever Bhirendra erred in his ritual undertakings, forgetting a *mantra* or performing something incorrectly, his grandfather would come to him in his sleep and slap his hands.

Bhirendra believes he never really had a choice in becoming a *bombo*; his calling dictated his career. Had he refused the call, he would have sickened and died, possibly becoming entirely mad and committing suicide, or not being able to stop shaking. Thus the shamanizing itself is conceived as a cure.

Experiences similar to that reported by Bhirendra have also been reported by shamans from many other cultures. The psychopathology of these critical experiences is often noted. For example, Sternberg (1925:474) mentions that the election of the shaman is manifested by the outbreak of a serious illness, usually at the onset of sexual maturity. Czaplicka (1914:172) writes that, among the Tungus of the Trans-Baikal region, "To be called to become a shaman is generally equivalent to being afflicted with hysteria."

In fact, there seems to be general agreement that the shaman, during the critical calling, suffers from some form of psychopathology although there are various opinions as to what this illness is. Both Eliade (1964:27), Ackerknect (1943:46), as well as the Tamang, maintain that the shaman's initial experience (the calling) is equivalent to an affliction from which recovery is expected. However, there is much argument in the literature over whether or not cure does occur (cf. Devereux 1956:28-29; Lot-Falck 1970). Silverman (1967:22-23) compares such experiences to acute schizophrenia. In this form, the schizophrenia is merely one life episode, happening abruptly and leading to a non-paranoid resolution. This is opposed to another "reactive" form, one which leads to a paranoid solution in which the inner experience is not comprehended and the individual prematurely redirects his attention to the external world because of his terror of the inner. The acute shamanic experience, on the other hand, is supposed to bring about a psychological readjustment of the individual. The shaman, as Silverman (1967:23) says, is a "healed madman."

The process of becoming cured can be compared to Wallace's (1961:182-184) concept of "mazeway resynthesis," i.e., a reorganization of one's way of structuring the world due to intolerable anxiety and crisis. Although the experience is critical, its outcome (psychological change and attainment of a vocation) seems highly therapeutic. Prince (1976:127) suggests that the type of psychotic experience undergone by the shaman parallels the therapeutic experience in that it breaks down rigid ego structures and reconstitutes them.

Bateson (1961:x-xiv) believes that the acute psychotic episode is sometimes part of a psychological process that leads to a resolution of a pathology situation. He compares it to the structure of an initiation ceremony, with the death and rebirth structure equivalent to the passage through psychosis. In other words, the "acute schizophrenic episode," once begun, is guided in its course by an "endogenous process" that leads from psychosis to a completion involving a return to the normal world with new insights. Similarly, Prince (1980:180) writes, "The function of psychosis is to break down the ego and its maladaptive defenses (explained as death or world destruction) and to reintegrate as an adaptive ego (experienced as a rebirth)."

Freud was probably the first to apply this type of thinking to psychotic syndromes. In his analysis of Scheber's *Memoirs of My Nervous Illness*, Freud (1953:347) suggests that paranoid disturbances should be looked upon as a dissolution of an overly rigid ego and an attempt at reconstruction which, in the case of the psychotic, is "never wholly successful." He writes, "The delusion formation, which we take to be a pathological product, is in reality an attempt at recovery, a process of reconstruction." However, why is it that some individuals are successful in resolving these crises and others less successful, developing delusionary and paranoid systems instead? One of the determining factors may well be the extent of socio-cultural acceptance of the crisis experience itself. Wallace (1961:182f) suggests that culture enters into the process by imposing certain evaluations upon experience. Thus culture can be either a hindrance or support to mazeway resynthesis, dependent on whether it views the experience as undesirable and negative, therefore invoking shame, anxiety and feelings of alienation, or as positive and appropriate, providing a culturally-sanctioned channel for non-ordinary experience. In other words, the status, role and prestige accorded the shaman greatly enhance his chances of successful readaptation as opposed to a similar acute experience in another culture where such supports are unavailable.

Although, as mentioned earlier, shamans as a group cannot be considered either normal or abnormal, it is important to view the "shaman's calling" *per se* from a psychological perspective because of the widespread occurrence of this type of experiential phenomenon. Bhirendra's experience is very much like other reported mystical or religious experiences. For example, the spark of light he saw is a common visual element in these experiences, as is the "dark night of the soul" before being "saved" (Underhill 1955:169-170). Bhirendra's religious experience occurred within the cultural context of shamanism, and as a result of the training embarked upon after the experience, Bhirendra found a vocation and meaning in his life.

The shaman does not live in an idiosyncratic universe nor does he suffer from an "impairment of reality testing," cognitive distortion or maladaptive behavior. The world of spirits, the dreams and visions of the shaman may seem abnormal from our cultural perspective. But from the perspective of the Tamang, it is all part of reality which consensus populates with numerous spirits believed to possess individuals, cause illness and exist in other demonstrable ways. Seen from such a culturally relative point of view, shamanism is not a pathological delusion but is comparable to what Spiro (1965) calls a "culturally constituted defense." The shaman's training is a set of psychotherapeutic techniques designed to channel and guide the chaotic feelings created during the calling into a culturally constituted pattern.

The Initiatory Levels

After the calling, all Tamang shamans must find a guru in order to be initiated, a process involving the learning of a body of myths and the mastery of ritual methods and techniques, including trance states. In my relationship with Bhirendra and his five disciples, I observed that the guru functions as a psychotherapist in that he explains to his trainees the meaning of their dreams, hallucinations and paroxysms, and places them within the context of an intiatory system. The shaking becomes identified as the possession of an ancestor, and the visions and dreams related to mythology and other aspects of the belief system. It has frequently been noted that the shaman functions as a psychiatrist in relation to his patients (Lederer 1973; Levi-Strauss 1963; Moerman 1979). This is equally true in the relationship to his disciples.

Tamang shamanic training is didactic in that the shaman must learn hundreds of *mantra* and myths, ritual procedures and methods. In acquiring this knowledge, he learns many aspects of the belief system in depth, becoming a cultural expert.

Training also involves production and mastery of trance states. The guru conducts numerous *puja* in which the neophyte plays the drum in order to bring about possession or visionary states. At each of the major healing *puja*, the disciples sing the myths with the guru, and call on the gods to possess them. The idea behind these exercises is that the more one becomes entranced, the more control is gained over the trance state. Bhirendra mentioned many times that the more I played the drum and shook, the sooner the gods would talk through me and the more visions I would have. The goal is to become able to produce the trance state at will and control its duration.

There are four stages to the Tamang shaman's initiation. Each initiatory grade represents a higher attainment by the neophyte. The calling is considered the initial stage. Here possession is unsolicited. The initiant's condition in this stage is described as "crazy possession."

The second stage (Ta: *lha khreba*)[1] begins with the training of the disciple by the human guru who prepares him for performance of *guru puja*, in which the possessing spirit (the tutelary guru) speaks out and identifies itself through the disciple. Bhirendra explained that, during the ceremony, the human guru first plays the drum and becomes possessed by various of the neophyte's ancestors. During each possession, the guru attempts to transfer the spirit to the initiant, accomplished either by passing the beating drum to him or by using two drums, if available. The neophyte may shake mildly with each transfer until the proper spirit, the one who has specifically chosen the disciple all along, is transferred. Then the initiant shakes violently, and the possessing entity speaks, identifying itself. Thus *guru puja* is done to formally identify the possessing agent that made the neophyte mad, and the identification is made through the initiant himself. This spirit then assumes the function of *mukhiya guru* (chief internal guru) and, if it has not already done so, it begins to visit the candidate in his dreams to introduce him to all the spirits over

[1] *Lha khreba* (Ta.) is the term most generally but indiscriminately used for all forms of possession. When shamans were queried in detail, the terms became specific to initiatory levels and types of possession, *lha khreba* being one form.

whom the dead shaman had gained mastery in his lifetime. This progresses simultaneously with the *bombo*'s didactic training.

So, in the second stage, one develops more control over the possessed state. The disciple begins to learn how to call on his tutelary guru to possess him voluntarily. The neophyte still shakes uncontrollably, however, and at times mumbles inconsistencies. This stage is described as being "ridden by the guru," or "having the guru upon one's shoulders." Although possession is induced and ended with the help of the human guru, possession still cannot be suitably controlled in order to be used by the shaman in complex ritualistic situations.

In the third stage of initiation, an even more controlled form of possession (Ta: *lha khresi*) is attained. Here the *bombo* initiant gains control over the gods and is therefore able to utilize his powers in the performance of ritual duties. In this stage, the tutelary guru speaks coherently through the shaman, and not only to identify itself. There are no more ramblings, laughing or one-word utterances. The *bombo* can now perform diagnosis and other types of divination. With the aid of the gods and spirits over which he has gained control, and through the ritual methods and myths learned from the guru, he can perform healing *puja*. The initiant is now a shaman. In fact, many *bombo* never progress beyond this level. This is the stage of control which, as noted in Chapter 1, is so important in distinguishing pathological from controlled possession. The *bombo* expresses this distinction by saying that he is now "riding the guru," indicating that the relationship has changed: the shaman is now master of the spirits and thus of the affliction initially caused him.

It is interesting to note that the initiant's progress from second to third (and fourth) levels corresponds to shamanic beliefs about the three souls of men which are thought to be located (1) in the solar plexus, (2) heart, and (3) top of the head. The shaking of a *bombo* is said to be brought about through the lower soul (Ta: *sem chang*). This lower soul embodies the power of anger, which is utilized by the *bombo* in sorcery. When an individual dies, this soul may stay on earth and cause trouble as a *lagu*. When a neophyte first becomes possessed, it is this soul that is activated, and it is the first he must come to master. This is done through the heart soul (Ta: *yidam bhla*), the soul of compassion and of speech, which is activated when the chief tutelary spirit speaks through the initiant while possessing him.

The third soul (Ta: *che wa*) is described as a light located between the eyes. It is the light of consciousness and also the light that shines from the eyes. Further, when it is controlled, the shaman is said to have attained the highest power one can get through initiations (Ta: *thuisal bhorba*).[2] Literally, *thuisal* means "loss of consciousness," *bhorba* "to take away"; at this stage the *che wa* soul of the *bombo* can embark on magical flight. That is, the shaman is able to soul journey to the heavens and underworlds (see Figure 1). At this level, unripe or "crude visions" (Ta: *ta rang ga*) are superseded by "clear visions" (Ta: *ta top che*).

This final initiatory goal is achieved in two stages, marked by two ceremonies: (Ta.) *pho wang lung* and *gufa* (Ta: *cham*) or cave. *Pho* is a concept with many related meanings. Bhirendra often identified it with the *che wa* soul; other times with the tuft of hair worn by shamans at the crown of their heads, in the same spot as the *mukhiya guru* resides to protect the shaman. *Pho* is sometimes said to be the *mukhiya guru*'s *śakti*. In order for the *che wa* soul to leave the body, the heavenly doors (*swarga dhokaa*) located atop the head at the fontanelle must be opened. At the time of death, the *bombo*'s characteristic tuft of hair is pulled forward to the *swarga dhokaa* so that the *che wa* soul can leave the *bombo*'s body and travel with his tutelary spirit to heaven where the *bombo*'s deeds and misdeeds are evaluated in order to determine his future rebirth. This ritual act is known as "removing the *pho*." The same ritual manipulation is repeated during *pho wang lung puja*, and it has the same meaning, allowing the *bombo* to soul journey, protected and accompanied by his *mukhiya guru*. Thus there is an equation of the separation of the soul at death

[2] The Tamang term *lhari nyiba* (cf. Höfer 1974:177,182) and *lha den cham nyiba* (both meaning "to go along with the gods") were used interchangeably with *thuisal bhorba*.

THE HEAVENLY DEITIES

HEAVENS

9	Dawa
8	Tagiyama Chenpo
7	Lung Ghesar Gyalpo
6	Chandra Jogini
5	Shira Jogini
4	Vajra Jogini
3	Tara Jogini
2	Bichuwa Dhana Dhameni
1	Akasa Tara Mandala

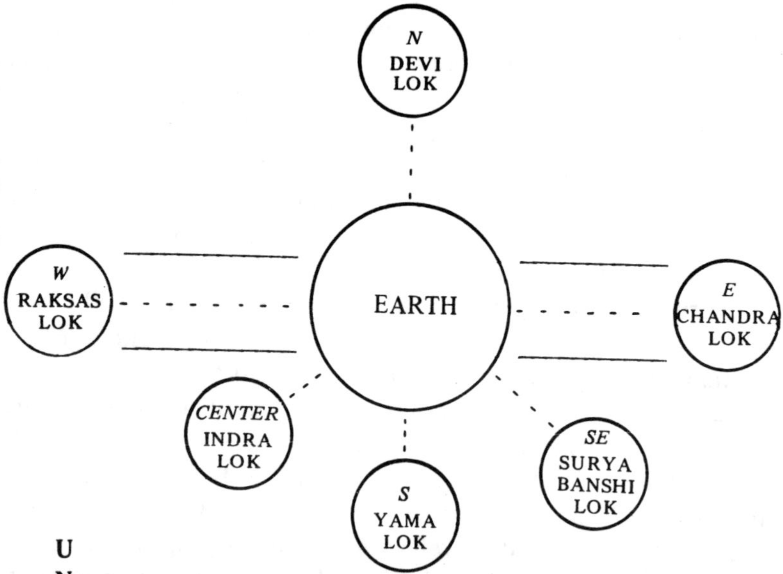

UNDERWORLDS

1	Dharma Raja
2	Gopiye Raja
3	Betya Raja
4	Bansiya Raja
5	Henenmena Raja
6	Jetemede Raja
7	Ding Raja
8	Jala Raja
9	Ses Nag Raja

THE UNDERWORLD DEITIES

Figure 1

13. A shaman on magical flight, lying on the ground as his soul journeys to the heavens.

and during initiation. After *pho wang lung puja*, the initiant is said to "have attained *pho*" and thereby to have clear visions.

Gufa is the *bombo*'s final initiation. Essentially, it is the climb to highest heaven.[3] Although *gufa* means cave in Nepali, the *gufa* is not really a cave. Rather it is a hollow shelter made of rice straw, which is perched atop four tall stilts and normally used to store grain. For *gufa*, Bhirendra explained that it is erected in a cemetery and decorated all over with hundreds of white "soul flowers" or *narling mendo* (*bignoniaceae oroxylum indicum*). Leading up to the *gufa* is a nine-rung ladder. The ladder serves as *axis mundi*,[4] i.e., it leads to the heavens, with each of the nine rungs corresponding to a level of heaven. *Gufa* initiation takes place above the ninth level. The initiation lasts seven days during which the initiant *bombo*, dressed in a ritual white frock and peacock-feather headdress, continually plays the drum. The little food and water he consumes is brought to him by his guru, who does not speak to him after the first day. On the first day, the guru stays in the *gufa* with the neophyte. They practice repeating the *mantra* the initiant will need to call on the gods and fight off the evil spirits he will confront. They play the drum all day and night, singing and calling on the gods to possess them. The process is repeated by the neophyte alone for the remainder of the time. During these days and nights spent alone, the initiant has visions of ghosts and spirits which he masters. On the seventh day, before leaving the *gufa*, Bhirendra had the following vision in which he journeyed to the highest heaven and saw the supreme, deity of the shamans, Ghesar Gyalpo:

[3] Eliade (1964:259ff) mentions that, in cultures the world over where shamanism is practiced, there is a concept of a central axis (sometimes conceived to be a pole, ladder, bridge, and often a tree) connecting the various levels of the universe, and that traversing these levels is possible because they are linked together by this axis.

[4] Ritual climbs symbolizing ascent to heaven, according to Watters (1975) are part of the initiation ceremonies of the Kham Magars, another Tibetan group in Nepal (cf. Hitchcock 1968).

> I walked into a beautiful garden with flowers of many different colors. There was also a pond and golden glimmering trees. Next to the pond was a very tall building which reached up into the sky. It had a golden staircase of nine steps leading to the top. I climbed the nine steps and saw Ghesar Gyalpo at the top, sitting on his white throne. He was dressed in white and his face was all white. He had long white hair and a white crown. He gave me milk to drink and told me that I would attain much *śakti* to be used for the good of my people.

Bhirendra relates that he left the *gufa* and returned to his village. On his way back, he met many villagers who had come out to meet him along with his guru. They carried him back to the village cheering. This kind of social support, as noted earlier, is an important psychological factor for the fulfillment of the shaman's vocation. Tamang culture provided an idiom for the articulation of Bhirendra's experience; it rendered it an event by casting it into the world of meaning and thereby constituting a basis for action.

Tantric Yoga and Tamang Shamanism

There are historical connections between shamanism and Hindu-Buddhist yoga practices. In fact, the Siberian Tungus term *śaman* (shaman) derives from the South, and its original meaning is "ascetic, one who practices austerities." The religious practices associated with such holy men stimulated and influenced the development of the more ancient Northern Asiatic shamanism (Eliade 1964:498; Mironov and Shirokogoroff 1924:130, n.52; Shirokogoroff 1935:282). This influence and stimulation is even more obvious among the Tamang, who have assimilated many of the concepts of Hindu and Buddhist Tantra while retaining their essential animistic and shamanic belief system. That is, they have reinterpreted and given other values to certain Tantric yoga practices that are now intimately connected to their shamanic religion.

The most obvious of these influences is in the parallel between the Tamang concept of three souls and the Tantric yoga concept of *cakra* (Skt.), the centers of energy located at various points between the base of the spine and the top of the head. Yogic stages of initiation are marked by the yogi's ability to move this energy, described as a coiled serpent (Skt: *kuṇḍalinī*) in Hindu practice and air-wind/vital force (Tib: *lung*) by the Buddhists, up a channel located in the spinal column to the top of the head (Skt: *sahasrara cakra*) or "crown center" (see Evans-Wentz 1958: 32,189f; Govinda 1960:140ff; Woodroffe 1974:103ff). Similarly, in the Tamang system, the lower levels of initiation correspond to the activation of lower souls located at lower levels in the body. The highest level of initiation involves the *che wa* soul, located in the forehead between the eyebrows, which leaves the body through the top of the head to travel to the uppermost level of the universe where the highest god resides.

In Hindu Tantric yoga, the seventh *cakra* or crown center does not belong to the plane of the body; it is the plane of transcendence beyond time, space and material existence. This is why Woodroffe (1974) writes of the "six" *cakra* and of "bodiless consciousness." The realization of enlightenment is the attainment of this seventh *cakra* when the *kuṇḍalinī*, having ascended through the lower *cakra*, penetrates the uppermost *cakra* producing enstasis (Skt: *samādhi*) (see Eliade 1958a:37,243-246; Govinda 1960:143; Woodroffe 1974:428f). The experience of arousing the *kuṇḍalinī* to the crown center is described as yielding to an "out-of-the-body" type experience (Krishna 1971:11,69,155).

To a large extent, yoga has "somaticized" the symbolism and rites of shamanism. The *axis mundi* so typical of shamanism, the ladder reaching through the numerous levels of heaven, corresponds in Tantric yoga to the spinal column and the *cakra* which are likewise traversed in order to attain the final initiatory experience. The Tamang shaman's activation of the three souls, as undertaken at different levels of initiation, culminates in the ritual ascent to heaven during *gufa*, and parallels the ascent of the *kuṇḍalinī* in Tantric yoga.

Tantric yoga and shamanism also both involve the "embodiment" of gods. The shaman becomes possessed by spirits whom they master; the master yogi "identifies" with gods representative of universal forces to the extent of becoming one with them and thereby comes to utilize these forces (Beyer 1973:66-69; Stabelein 1976:368). Furthermore, the initiatory experiences of shamans have many parallels in the experiences undergone by yogis in the process of awakening and raising the *kuṇḍalinī*. For example, Gopi Krishna (1971:63-67) describes himself as being terror stricken, fearing his own death, "shivering as if stricken with ague," before being saved by a "glowing radiance." All of this is strikingly similar to what is described in shamanic trance.

Enstasis or *samādhi* may be achieved through visionary and non-visionary states (cf. Fischer 1972). In the *Yoga-sūtras*, Patanjali distinguished between "*samādhi* with support" and "*samādhi* without support". That is, enstasis (invulnerability to external stimuli) can be accomplished by fixing one's thoughts on an internal object or idea (Eliade 1969:90f,109f), and this may entail a visionary state. In both Hindu and Buddhist Tantra "visualizations" are important at all stages of initiation (Bharati 1975:215; Govinda 1960:104f; Tucci 1961:68f). At the higher initiatory levels, imagery becomes mastered in both yoga and shamanism.

The shaman's visions are produced differently from the yogi's in that they are not developed from concentration on icons, *mandala* (Skt.), or other symbols upon which one fixes full attention. Yet for both practitioners, the images become part of an unfolding process, dreamlike creations that must be mastered. Like the shaman initiant, "the meditator cannot escape from the mysterious impulses of his own subconscious . . . which takes form in these images . . . instincts which had been repressed" (Tucci 1961:74-75).

As mentioned before, the shaman's trance is further distinguished from *samādhi* in that there is communicative rapport between shaman and audience during trance rituals. They are similar in that both systems employ techniques designed to produce altered states of consciousness as part of a discipline for self-development. Still, the psychological and social goals are quite distinct. Shamanic religion and psychology does not strive for the attainment of *nirvāṇa*, or to lead others to worldly detachment; it aims at gaining power to aid clients in overcoming their illnesses and other misfortunes.

Structure and Symbol in the Shaman's Training

Gufa follows the tripartite schemata of all rites of passage, as formulated by van Gennep (1908): separation, transition, and incorporation. The time Bhirendra spent in the *gufa* can be likened to what Turner (1969:97) terms the "liminal" phase of initiation rituals, in which status and role are temporarily suspended. This liminal or transitional phase is characterized by its "anti-structure." Liminality is defined by Turner as an undifferentiated state "betwixt and between" social distinctions, categories, and other things which separate people. The initiant in the liminal phase is at once no longer classified and not yet classified. Thus liminality has a paradoxical two-fold character: unstructured yet prestructured (Turner 1967a:96-98).

The symbols of death that appear in liminality represent the unstructured aspect. At the time of his calling, the Tamang neophyte shaman runs out into a cemetery; likewise for *gufa*, the ritual structure is set up in a cemetery. The cemetery is foreboding and dangerous–the place where the "undead" reside. The undead (*lagu*) are responsible for sickness and death. By going into the cemetery, the initiant opens himself up to attack and risks his life. The undead are also impure, placing the shaman initiant in an impure state in which no one, not even his guru (after the first day), is allowed to approach him. Mary Douglas (1972:200-201) asserts that what is "unclear" from the perspective of social categories, is generally considered to be polluting. *Lagu* fit this description in that they are neither dead nor alive. While they do not partake in the activities of the living, they continue to linger around the home of the living affecting their lives.

The prestructured aspect of the liminal period is also represented in *gufa*. The *gufa*, erected in the midst of the "undead," is covered all over with *narling mendo* flowers, symbols of life and rebirth. The *narling mendo* is a "dominant symbol" in Tamang culture: a single form with numerous cultural meanings including positive qualities, norms and values respected by the Tamang (cf. Turner 1967b:28-32). The *narling mendo* is a symbolic representation of purity. The *gufa* covered in flowers in the cemetery symbolizes purity in the midst of the impure (see below).

Within the *gufa*, the shaman meets the forces which seek his death. If they triumph over him, he will die within it. If he succeeds, he overcomes the last initiatory ordeal of a shaman: he meets the highest god on the highest level of heaven and receives power. Thus the *gufa* is a coincidence of opposites, a symbol uniting disparate natures. As Turner (1967a:99) says, "The coincidence in a single representation characterizes the peculiar unity of the liminal: that which is neither this nor that, yet is both." *Gufa* is neither womb nor tomb but both.

Thus the Tamang shaman must confront death and be reborn. This experience, as explained by Bhirendra, is very similar to what Turner (1974:47) calls *communitas*. He writes, "*Communitas* is most evident in liminality." It is a matter of "giving recognition to an essential and generic human bond, without which there could be no society" (Turner 1969:97). It is similar to Durkheim's (1915:469) "effervescence," a state of emotional arousal from which is generated the common feeling of groupness, the foundation of social structure. It is also similar to Goldschmidt's (1959: 26ff) inborn "need for positive affect" which presages man's sociability, and is indispensable to the functioning of the social system. Thus *communitas* has an "existential quality"; "it involves the whole man in his relation to other whole men" (Turner 1969:127).

It is this existential quality of humanness and feeling of brotherhood that I believe Bhirendra realized in his *gufa* initiation. At the liminal period, he was no longer an individual against other individuals. What was important was the interrelatedness between others. Bhirendra's vision and message from Ghesar Gyalpo was unselfish. It was not that he was set apart but that he was granted powers to relieve the suffering of others, a power which created a bond between him and his people.

When Bhirendra tried to explain his *gufa* experience, he was always at a loss to express his feelings. It had that ineffable nature often attributed to the realization of mystical experiences. But the tears which welled up in his eyes, the sound in his voice, they told that it was a most significant experience in his life. The shamanic initiation rituals and the *communitas* they evoke are existential and psychological, and from his experience with them, Bhirendra's entire life was changed. His vision became the model or pattern for a "mazeway resynthesis." "The new shaman," as Bourguignon (1976b:10) writes, "has not 'recovered', that is, has not reestablished an earlier equilibrium or pattern of functioning, but rather has become 'transformed' both in personality and in social status and role."

Spirit Possession: Psychopathology and Psychotherapy

As discussed in Chapter 1, shamanic trance is inclusive of magical flight, spirit possession, and other interpretations of trance. Further, the altered state is controlled and utilized in community context. Additionally, it was noted that shamans typically are in communicative rapport with both patient and audience during trance performances. Yet another psychological component of the shaman's trance is the element of memory (Peters and Price-Williams 1980).

Loss of memory for trance states is generally considered to be a "dissociative reaction" and therefore psychopathological. The original meaning of dissociation derives from pathology, coming from Janet's (1907) and Charcot's (1889) studies of hysteria, hypnosis and multiple personality. The basic theory of dissociation originated in Charcot's belief that the stream of consciousness splits up into diverse elements in hysterical and hypnoid phenomena. Janet, who first used the term, viewed dissociation as the converse of the then-prevalent theory of association. That is, if memories are brought to consciousness via association, then memories not available to association are dissociated. Janet further postulated that these unconscious thoughts form integrated subsystems, or even secondary personalities, which alternate with normal consciousness. This definition of dissociation, emphasizing "compartmentalization" and "amnesia," persists in contemporary psychiatry (English and English 1958:159; West 1967:890).

Shamanic spirit possession has often been viewed as mental pathology and is commonly thought to be a dissociative reaction. The symptoms (shaking seizures, distorted physiognomy, alternating personalities, *et al.*) are too close to the classic hysteria, as described by Charcot (1889) and Janet (1907) and later psychoanalyzed by Freud, to escape the scrutiny of numerous investigators of shamanism. Oesterreich (1966:26f,40f; orig.1921), however, shows that possession trances may be either "lucid" or "somnambulistic." In the former, there is memory upon awakening and consciousness during the trance; in the latter form there is amnesia. The view that possession-trance and amnesia are not necessarily connected is confirmed by Hilgard (1978:18) who, in his "neo-dissociation" theory, says that possession represents a special type of dissociation in which "amnesias are not essential." He (1978: 248-252) emphasizes that repression and dissociation are not interchangeable terms. As far as shamanic possession (voluntary and controlled) is concerned, Peters and Price-Williams (1980) report that memory of trance states is the rule in 20 of 29 cultures in which shamans become spirit possessed. Further, in at least two of the cultures where amnesia is reported by shamans, cultural beliefs about what "authentic" possession is seems to be the reason why amnesia is reported rather than what actually occurs psychologically.

West (1967:890) indicates that dissociation is not necessarily psychopathological. In fact, some investigators maintain that dissociation is potentially beneficial. For example, Bourguignon (1965:55-56) discussed the healing aspect of dissociation. From her observations of Haitian possession trance, she writes of "dissociation in the service of the self," which is compared to Kris's (1952:253) "functional regression," i.e., a trance or other similar mental state (free association, psychodrama, reverie, etc.) where ego functions are relaxed and inspring, insightful or psychotherapeutic experiences follow. Bourguignon (1965:56) argues that, in Haitian Voodoo, spirit possession is a "self-enhancing" experience increasing the "field of action" and "scope for fulfillment."

As noted earlier, Tamang shamans discern different types of possession. The initial calling is non-amnesiac and involuntary, a trance "emically" interpreted as illness. Shamanic possession, the result of successful initiation, is controlled, remembered and nonpathological, according to the Tamang. The diagnoses performed while in the possessed state are part of a dramatic social performance that impresses and awes observers with respect to the shaman's mastery and power. Ritual success leads in turn to prestige in the world outside of the ritual context. In other words, shamanic possession trance is culturally respected and self-enhancing.

Yap (1960:126-129) distinguishes two types of possession based on the positive or negative value assigned by the individual and/or his culture to the possession state. If the phenomenon is viewed negatively by others and censured by the rest of the self system, a dissociation occurs marked by loss of memory. The other form of possession is called "mythopoetic." The ideas attached to this type of possession differ from the other in that they reflect positive cultural values and are therefore unrepressed. Typically, these include possessions by deities, culture heroes or other respected personages.

Jung. (1969b:304f; 1962:110f) also believed that there are forms of possession that do not involve repression. These are the emergence of autonomous complexes or archetypes out of the collective unconscious that had not previously been conscious and therefore could not have been repressed. Archetypes reflect man's inner duplicity and consequently take the form of mythical heroes and devils. Jung, however, gives scant attention to the consequences of personal and cultural beliefs and how these influence and shape conscious acceptance or rejection of the possession trance.

The type of possession found in Tamang shamanism is of the mythopoetic variety. The shaman reacts to his crisis (or calling), not through repression and dissociation, but through possession and identification with a culturally accepted role model. Bhirendra's case is typical in that his *mukhiya guru*, who possesses him and whose role he imitates, was a respected shaman and ancestor. The Tamang do not consider this pathological. And, as Yap (1960: 126-127) indicates, possession by an "accessory mythical personality" may be psychotherapeutic in that it " . . . can help the individual to grasp a profoundly complex life situation, as a first step towards further action and self development."

Sargent (1973:4-17) points out that abreactive or cathartic states parallel possession states and that the latter have the same therapeutic effect as the former. Commenting on the shamans' trance states and their psychological implications, Levi-Strauss (1977:452) posits that the shaman is a "professional abreactor" in that he relives the origin of his disturbances (i.e., the calling) each time he becomes entranced, until it is ultimately overcome. Seen in this way, the shaman's initiatory process, in which the neophyte performs numerous rituals in which he plays the drum in order to induce possession trance, has the therapeutic effect of reinvoking the initial possession and the emotions associated with this experience. While there is not an exact verbal recall of the precipatory event (the calling) during the Tamang shaman's initiatory altered state experiences, as is considered essential in the psychoanalytic technique of abreaction (Breuer and Freud 1955:6), the neophyte shaman discharges powerful affects by crying, laughing, trembling, and the like. Now, as Scheff (1979: 77) concludes from his review of Freud's early theory and treatment of hysteria, and the more recent literature on cathartic therapy, the crux of the theory of catharsis involves the discharge of repressed emotions like grief, fear, anger and embarrassment, and "verbal recall is neither necessary nor sufficient for therapy and emotional discharge is both necessary and sufficient."

I observed initiation ceremonies in which some of Bhirendra's disciples shook violently when possessed, alternately crying and laughing without apparent external cuase. At times they shouted fragment sentences. At one such ritual, a disciple cried out "Father!" several times while shaking violently. When the disciples manifested this sort of behavior, Bhirendra found it very difficult to establish rapport with them; i.e., they were unresponsive to his demands and did not return easily from the altered state. Bhirendra always demanded that the possessing spirit speak up and identify itself through the disciple. If this resulted, then the disciple's paroxysm would become less intense. These ceremonies, called purification rituals, were performed sometimes twice a month or more by guru and disciples, and serve as a primary means by which higher initiatory levels are achieved. The purification rituals are repeated numerous times before each major ceremony that leads to iniatory advancement; by performing them, the acumen to produce and control trance, so necessary for advancement, is attained by the neophyte.

It can be argued that psychoanalysis posits only one catharsis for each trauma and symptom, while Tamang initiations invoke repeated possessions. However, as Scheff (1979:75) maintains, what is required, and what psychoanalysis demonstrates through concepts like "abreaction of arrears," is that repeated discharge of the emotional tension associated with a trauma is necessary before the full quota of pathogenic affect is released.

Like contemporary psychoanalytical therapy, Tamang initiation involves "remembering, repeating and working through" of psychical disturbances (Freud 1958a). The neophyte shaman remembers his possession trances, and these are discussed with the guru. During these discussions, the altered state experience is amplified upon, and given a name, cause and purpose. Following the traditional pattern, the neophyte learns that his initial chaotic disturbance was possession caused by a respected ancestor who wants to bestow *śakti*, enabling the recipient to become a shaman. Thus there is memory of the calling. Eliade (1958b:102) writes, " . . . the shaman has succeeded in integrating into consciousness a considerable number of experiences . . . that are reserved for dreams (and) madness. . . . The shaman is the man that *knows* and *remembers*. . . . He is not solely an ecstatic but also a contemplative. . . . " Of course, "remembering," in the sense of psychoanalysis, is quite different than it is in Tamang shamanism. The latter is not reductive-analytic; paroxysms, dreams and other trance behaviors are not related to the individual's past. Tamang world view is much different. Their universe is personified and spirits are considered the causes of otherwise inexplicable events. Still, the initiant's possession and other trance experiences are not lost. They are interpreted by the guru and placed within the context of the shamanic belief system.

Freud (1953:455) asserted that one of the most important aspects of psychoanalysis is making the unconscious known by means of interpretation. However different in content the Freudian interpretations may seem to those given by the Tamang shaman guru, they are functionally equivalent in that they provide a rationale for disturbing experiences. That is, the interpretations in both systems explain otherwise confusing mental states and are therefore similar to what Marmor (1962:289-290) calls "therapeutic insight." He writes, "What we call insight is essentially the conceptual framework by means of which a therapist establishes . . . a logical relationship between events, feelings or experiences that seem unrelated in the mind of the patient." What I am suggesting is that the shaman's rationale is as psychotherpeutically effective as the rationale or theory of any other school of thought used to organize confusing mental states and thereby provide insight. In other words, insight is a culturally relative term. The belief cited by Kiev (1964:27) that "primitive" psychotherapy provides "remission without insight" and is therefore not a psychological cure, because it does not entail introspective insight into psychoanalytical concepts, is ethnocentric. As Levi-Strauss (1963:192-193) writes, "That the mythology of the shaman does not correspond to objective reality does not matter." Similarly, J. Frank (1973:224) writes, " . . . an interpretation need not be correct but merely plausible," and that "faith" in the doctor's theory, rather than "truth" of the interpretation, is of therapeutic importance (see Torrey 1972:14-16).

The shaman guru, like other psychotherapists, provides a "language" that allows for the organization of otherwise meaningless mental states. This "meaning-scheme," as Fingarette (1963: 22-27) suggests, is more than just words and concepts. It contains affective and experiential aspects that satisfy a basic human "drive toward meaning," the fulfillment of which is synonymous with the therapeutic goal of ego integration. Seen in this way, the purpose of psychoanalysis, which is to transform mental illness through meaning ("Where id was, there shall ego be"), is very similar to Tamang initiatory psychotherapy which likewise provides meaning and ego integration to diffuse mental states.

The disciple "repeats" his initial crisis, the symptoms of shaking, the anxiety (i.e., his "crazy possession") in the presence of the guru numerous times. According to Freud (1958a:150-153), repetition or "acting out" of traumatic events, even in disguised form within the analytical situation, is crucial to therapy, although it may lead to a temporary "exacerbation of symptoms." It is therapeutic because it also leads to recollection and thereby symptom mastery if the patient has the courage to face his disturbance " . . . which has a solid ground for its existence and out of which things of value for his future life have to be discovered." This is precisely what is conveyed to the Tamang neophyte. He is compelled to find value in his disturbance, to master it and utilize it in his profession.

Freud (1961a:194) maintained that catharsis remained a significant element in the development of psychoanalysis. The cathartic element is most prominent in the "working through" phase of psychoanalysis in which the analysand, in the process of overcoming his resistances to the repressed, experiences strong emotions which Freud (1958a:155-156) believed is equivalent to an abreaction of the strangulated affects. The shaman disciple also emotionally works through his resistances to repeating and remembering his initial crisis when he reexperiences possession in sessions with the guru until it ceases to have an overwhelming affect, and the calling can then take on meaning and purpose in his life.

Thus the series of initiations undertaken by the shamans contain numerous elements similar to contemporary psychotherapy. In fact, the Tamang initiatory system is equivalent to a psychotherapy. What is more, passage not only constitutes cure but the adoption of a profession, and therefore it represents the Tamang variant of "training analysis."

Magical Flight, Lucid Dreams and Psychotherapy

In Tamang shamanism, magical flight, a visionary type of trance, is mastered on the fourth initiatory level. The first three involve increasing control of the possession state. The visions that occur during the calling, and those which arise spontaneously during the purification rituals are called crazy visions. Those which arise when the shaman has gained the capacity to voluntarily enter into visionary trance and, to a certain extent, have control over its contents, are known as clear visions. As mentioned earlier, the ability to have clear visions is attained after the "heavenly door" is opened. Once this occurs, the neophyte is said to be able to soul travel throughout the cosmos (Figure 1).

Seto, Bhirendra's most advanced disciple, reached the third initiatory level, having had his heavenly door opened, but had not yet progressed to *gufa*. At one healing ritual, Seto was playing the drum and shaking when he rose and began to dance in a frenzied manner. After a few minutes, he fell to the ground and lay there; trembling slightly, he related a vision wherein a god advised him of the causes and circumstances of the patient's illness. All of this is customary behavior when a shaman embarks on a soul journey. However, before Seto could return to his normal state, he was attacked by the god. He screamed "no, no!" and writhed on the ground, enacting the struggle which was taking place in his vision. Bhirendra called to him, threw rice on him (a ritual gesture used to dispel a possession state). Still Seto was unreachable and out of control. A few minutes later, the paroxysms subsided slightly. Bhirendra quickly lit a small candle and placed it in Seto's mouth. Seto swallowed it. Shortly afterwards, Seto returned to the waking state and told everyone that the god had grown angry with him and attacked him. Bhirendra further explained that when he gave Seto the candle, he empowered him with the *śakti* of fire and thereby enabled him to get free of the god.

Control of visionary trance is learned in the purification rituals, just as possession trance is mastered in the earlier stages. The ultimate object of these purification ceremonies is for the tutelary spirit, the disciple, and the guru to travel together to

Devi Lok (see the cosmic map in Figure 1) in order to receive a blessing from the goddess there. I witnessed Bhirendra and Seto performing this ritual. They sat on the floor and played their drums while shaking violently. They bounced high, perhaps two or three feet into the air from their cross-legged positions, as though they were seated upon springs. Another of Bhirendra's disciples sprinkled the shamans with flowers and water from a sacred vessel that had been prepared earlier. When the trance ended, Seto described a vision in which he, Bhirendra, and their tutelary gurus traveled to Devi Lok, and received a blessing of flowers and water from the goddess, just as had occurred during the ritual. Bhirendra reported the same vision.

This training appears to have the purpose of creating a specific introspective state, one in which the neophyte learns to enter voluntarily, a visionary state in which he is participant, observer, and controller. That is, while the shaman organismically participates in his visions, even to the extent of occasionally miming some of his encounters, he is able to stand back, so to speak, and manipulate his visionary contents.

Bhirendra said he was both aware of himself as a participant in a ritual and, at the same time, involved in another world invisible to others. This simultaneous awareness of ego and dream ego is known in the literature as "lucid dreaming." Lucid dreaming is a state in which the dreamer is aware that he is dreaming and that his experiences are different from the ordinary experiences of waking life. Tart (1977:176) describes the lucid dream as a state " . . . in which you feel as if you 'wake up' in terms of mental functioning within the dreamworld; that is, you feel as rational and as in control of your mental state as you do in your ordinary state of consciousness, but you are still experientially located within the dreamworld." Thus, in this state, the individual has the ability to be both rational and produce images simultaneously. Price (1968:7), another scientific researcher of this phenomenon, similarly emphasizes the experience of dream control when he writes that the "most interesting feature of lucid dreams is that the dreamer, once he has noticed that he is dreaming, has some degree of voluntary control over the subsequent course of his dream."

There are only a few ways mentioned in the literature in which these states may occur spontaneously in dreams. Frederick van Eeden (1969:153; orig.1913), an early pioneer in the study of lucid dreams, reports that flying or floating in dreams often initiates lucidity. Nightmares are another common type of lucid dream (Green 1968:45). One reason why these types of dreams may initiate the awareness that one is dreaming is because of the unusual, or strikingly unreal nature of the experience, a situation prone to producing a critical thought and the realization that one must be dreaming.

Lucidity may be established from the waking state or from the dream state. As indicated, lucidity can be initiated by awakening critical or analytical functions which are in abeyance in other types of dreams. In the waking state, lucidity may be produced by relaxing and letting dream images surge forth while maintaining awareness that one is dreaming. Such a technique was employed by Ouspensky (1960:272-273) in his self experiments designed to observe dream processes. The mental state that resulted from such practices were called "half-dream states" because he seemed to be awake (conscious of self) and dreaming simultaneously.

Lucid dreams have also been likened to "out-of-the-body" experiences. Green (1968:20) writes that " . . . out-of-the-body experiences must be regarded as philosophically indistinguishable from lucid dreams." In both states, the individual recognizes at the time that he is in a state different from normal waking life. Oliver Fox (1962:34-38), who has written about his out-of-the-body experiences, emphasizes that there are various degrees of realization of consciousness during lucid dreams. States with a high degree of dual consciousness are termed "out-of-the-body" experiences or "astral projections." For example, Fox (1962:71) describes a dream in which he was vividly aware of being in bed and, at the same time, aware that he was walking by the sea in a dream.

Control over the imagery content in lucid dreams, as stated above, is often mentioned, although there may also be certain limitations. Marquis Hervey de Saint-Denis (1823-1892), whose exceedingly difficult to find text, *Dreams and the Means to Direct*

Them, is described by Ellenberger (1970:306-307) as "extensive" and "thorough," writes of only partial control. For example, he wanted to dream about his own death and several times directed his dream to take him to the top of a tower. Each time, however, after he jumped, he found himself with the spectators below, watching the man who had jumped from the tower. Van Eeden (1969:150-153), who also practiced controlling his lucid dreams, indicates that he gradually developed control over them as he became more proficient at producing them. Still, he could only give the dream a first impetus from which its content developed on its own accord, taking unexpected and strange turns.

It is often noted by lucid dreamers that emotional detachment is necessary in order to prolong dreams and retain lucidity. F.W.H. Myers (1887:241-242) writes that it is important to remain calm and avoid excitement in order to remain dreaming, and Fox (1962:43-44) writes that he found it necessary to maintain the role of an "impersonal observer." However, it is also possible to "lose oneself" in the dream, i.e., to continue dreaming but without lucidity, because of emotional quality. In this case, the critical attitude is lost and attention becomes submerged in the dream (Green 1968:100-101). Thus there appears to be a direct ratio between rational and controlled thought and the ability to prolong lucidity on the one hand, and the arousal of emotions, loss of critical stance and loss of lucidity on the other.

Half-dreams and other lucid states described in psychological and occult literature, with frequent images of flying and dual awareness to the point of believing that one is out-of-the-body, are extremely close to the descriptions Bhirendra provided of his trances, and reports from shamans the world over. The shaman's lucidity is obviously produced from the waking state. But unlike half-dreams, the shaman's trance is stimulated by drumming and other forms of hyperactivity. Still, the altered states produced seem very similar. Bhirendra described experiences that parallel classic out-of-the-body experiences. Beside his other-worldly travels (visions) and simultaneous awareness discussed earlier, Bhirendra also described "seeing" himself lying or sitting on the ground, while his "soul" followed a rainbow light upward.

Bhirendra seemed to exercise a high degree of control over his visions. For the most part, they were stereotyped. He traveled to specific heavens, encountered specific deities, and underwent similar experiences depending on the nature of the ritual he was performing. While he claimed to have visions which developed spontaneously, Bhirendra never lost his composure as Seto had. When asked if he ever lost control, Bhirendra replied that when he was learning and had crazy visions they were frequently frightening.

Shamanic lucid states are extremely similar to certain types of psychotherapy. In other words, the lucid states produced by shamans in their initiatory trials and during healing rituals are therapeutic and indeed may be an important means by which the shaman comes to master himself, i.e., become cured.

Shamanic possession-trance has already been compared to cathartic therapy and "dissociation in the service of the self," which were viewed as leading to a positive psychological and cultural readjustment. Magical flight, while employing different techniques, is also comparable to forms of psychotherapy. The Tamang shamans believe that the mastery of magical flight is a higher skill than mastery of possession trance, and that the latter must be mastered before work can begin on creating clear visions, which generally do not appear in the spirit possession states. Whether the Tamang ranking is psychologically important or not is difficult to judge. What seems signficant is that they have numerous initiatory techniques for creating psychological transformations, all of which have analogies in Western psychiatry.

Magical flight and the lucid dreams, which have been equated above, are extremely similar to numerous therapeutic techniques that make use of the patient's ability to visually imagine. These include C.G. Jung's (1969c) "active imagination," Desoille's (1966) "directed daydreams," Leuner's (1969) "guided affective imagery," Assagioli's (1976) "psychosynthesis," and others.

Freud (Breuer and Freud 1955:109-110, 153-154, 268ff) also made use of visual imagery with the "concentration" and "pressure" techniques he developed in the interim after he abandoned the use of hypnosis and before he adopted "free association." In the cases of Miss Lucy R. and Elizabeth von R., he described a technique in which the patients were instructed to lie down and close their eyes and concentrate on the meaning and origin of their symptoms. Freud found that the patients were able to produce memories and affects associated to their symptoms, in the form of mental images, when pressure was applied to their foreheads. Using this method, Freud was thus able to abandon dependence on hypnosis, without sacrificing the cathartic method. However, sometime before 1900, emphasis within psychoanalysis shifted from visual imagery to verbal association (Breuer and Freud 1955:268-271; Freud 1958b:101ff). Singer (1971) believes that this development was unfortunate due to the fact that imagery is emphasized in the daydream techniques of the European schools and in Reyher's (1963:457-458) "emergent uncovering" which states that "more primary process material" and associated affect can be correlated with experiences of visual imagery than from verbal associations.

Mary Watkins (1976) calls the psychotherapeutic visual imagery techniques "waking dreams" because they make use of the ego to record and observe the imaginal process. Therapeutic effectiveness is, of course, attributed to different factors by different psychological theories. Whereas Freud emphasized the memory and emotional discharge of a precipitating traumatic event in his pressure method, Desoille taught that imagery techniques are effective because they enable the patient to experience the collective background of his psyche, his "archetypes," and to participate with them in visions, thereby coming to "control" them and "lose fear of them" (Kretchmer 1969:224). In "directed daydreams", Desoille (1966:18-19,30f) suggests that the therapist guide the patient into a number of different imaginary scenes, the most important of which entail symbols of ascent and descent (climbing mountains, descending into caves, etc.). Obstacles confronted in these visions represent the patient's psychological complexes. By entering into the imagery, the therapist is able to help the patient overcome the negative images by suggesting certain symbols appropriate to the situation. No interpretation of symbols is attempted; Desoille and his followers take strong opposition to a reductive-analytic approach (see Van Den Berg 1962:14-17).

While obvious similarities exist between the Jungian point of view and that of Desoille, Singer (1974:72) points out that gross parallels also exist between directed daydreams and behavior modification techniques and that, on certain points, Desoille sounds very much like Wolpe. Singer (1974:72) writes, "The imagery serves also a desensitization function since the patient must confront . . . frightening figures . . . and is encouraged to remain in their presence while in a relaxed state and with the awareness that the therapist is at his side. Finally, there is a reeducation aspect in which under the relaxed conditions the patient can develop new patterns of responses."

The psychiatric techniques for producing waking dreams in clinical situations are, of course, very different from those occurring in Tamang shamanic initiation rites. Whereas the psychotherapist employs relaxing hypnotic meditative techniques, the shamans produce their states through rhythmic drum beating, shaking and frenetic dancing. In his imaginal states, the shaman confronts demons and gods, he ascends and descends the central axis to the nine levels of heavens and to the underworlds. Like the awake dreamer, he remains conscious and is aware of himself during his visions (i.e., lucid).

Psychotherapeutically speaking, the shaman sets up an inner dialogue between the characters which appear in his visions, representations of his unconscious, and his consciousness. According to Jung (1953:185; 1961:170-171), this type of dialogue is therapeutically beneficial because the images yield knowledge from which to proceed and include ways of knowing that are different, yet complementary to consciousness. This process of recognition of, and participation with, inner images that leads to the establishment of a collaborative relationship between the unconscious and the conscious ways of knowing is termed the "transcendent function" by Jung (1969), and it is an important technique in his type of psychotherapy. The inner dialogue is also considered important in "psychosynthesis" wherein an "inner master" (or teacher) appears in the visual imagery to provide answers to problems that the conscious personality does not feel it can solve by ordinary rational means (Assagioli 1976:202-207). Bhirendra's relationship with his *mukhiya guru* is extremely similar to the therapeutic inner dialogue suggested in these psychotherapies.

For the fully initiated shaman, "therapy" never ends. His initiations and healing rituals are his continuous therapy, functionally similar to the therapeutic benefit a psychotherapist receives from the psychotherapy he performs. In other words, healing rituals and initiations are therapeutic for patient, disciple and shaman alike. During them, the shaman continuously confronts his unconscious in the form of images. The successful shaman makes the encounter and transforms any threatening situation, just as is experienced in successful dream therapy. And while the shaman ostensibly acts in the service of his patient or disciple, his ego benefits from the very nature of his trance. As Leuner (1969:20) suggests " . . . the end result of successful confrontation is a strengthening of the ego."

Creative Illness and the Shamanic Vocation

It was discussed earlier that there are shamans who choose the profession and those, like Bhirendra, who are chosen through a calling. The calling is a critical experience causing the individual to become temporarily mad. The withdrawal from society, nights spent running through the forest naked, hallucinations, conversations with spirits, all these manifestations comprise the clinical picture of a severely disturbed individual. But the future shaman emerges from this "sickness" with important insights: a new vision of the world, a vocation, and personality transformation (i.e., a mazeway resynthesis). Ellenberger (1964; 1970:39,215,889) has classified such phenomena as "creative illnesses." In this group is also included the experiences of mystics, poets, philosophers and artists, among others. All have the same type of critical psychological experience in common, one that eventually leads to the psychological benefit of the individual. In fact, crisis experiences have been recognized by psychologists as catalysts to personal growth. Laski's (1961:160ff) description of "desolation experiences," and Bugental's (1965) of "existential crisis," states that although personal crisis can be negative and painful, it need not be pathological in that it can lead to new inner convictions, insights, and thereby benefit the individual. The value of crisis experience has been most emphatically stated by Forer (1963:280) who maintains that crisis experiences are part of many creative efforts, be they scientific, artistic, therapeutic or interpersonal.

Ellenberger (1970:889-890) distinguishes two types of creative illness. The first is that of the pathfinder, the other that of the follower. The former category includes those individuals who are the founders and teachers of new movements; that is, individuals who provide a practical guide for others to follow their original insights. Freud and Jung belong to this category as "both of them underwent a creative illness and . . . made it a model to be followed by their disciples under the name of training analysis." Followers are those who interpret their creative illness in the light of the pathfinders' models. In this category are those who seek spiritual guidance, like the shaman apprentice who must find a guru under whose instruction he overcomes and masters his initiatory sickness. Both categories, however, have in common the fact that the individual is convinced, once he recovers, that whatever he has discovered is a universal truth.

As already noted, the death and rebirth structure of acute schizophrenic experience, which I believe is just another term for creative illness, is similar to that of rites of passage. Like a rite of passage, these experiences invoke a psychological transformation and often lead to the development of a new vocation (artist, philosopher, shaman). The liminal period of "life crisis rituals" like rites of passage, which are said to be "anti-structural" paradoxical situations where all social classifiction and norms are suspended, sound like the chaotic and isolated situations in which the shaman finds himself during the critical period of his creative illness (e.g., the calling).

In the Tamang initiation scenario, it was shown that an

individual becomes a practicing shaman after he has mastered his spirit possession. This, however, does not end the training. If he had the calling, like Bhirendra, he suffered from visions in which he witnessed ghosts and demons devouring him. In the process of initiation, the shaman learns how to voluntarily produce the state that made him ill, to confront and ultimately control the forces that besieged him. While Bhirendra was miraculously saved by a white light in his calling, in his training he learned how to control his possessions and produce lucid visions where he met and mastered the evil spirits, causes of illness, that first attacked him.

During the liminal period of initiation, that is during *gufa* or the numerous purification rituals where the shaman attains altered states, the Tamang display numerous *narling mendo*, the flower described earlier as a "dominant symbol," and it plays a key psychological role in shaman's initiatory psychotherapy. Turner (1967b:28-30) and Ortner (1973:1339-1340) see such "key symbols" as playing a "summarizing" role by representing, in a single form, many of the norms and values of a culture. Comparable symbols in our culture are the cross and the flag. According to Turner (1967b:28-30), their principal function is to "transform the obligatory into the desirable." It is my hypothesis that dominant symbols serve as vehicles through which an individual's condition becomes transformed.

Dominant symbols are "preconscious," as Turner (1975: 175-176) points out, because they are cultural and available to consciousness even though the individual is only marginally aware of all their meanings at one and the same time. The *narling mendo* is actually one of hundreds of seeds, each sheathed in an opaque papery film, all of which are contained within a hard, large, curved brown pod. Because the inner seed is contained within its fragile shell, the *narling mendo* is also known as a "soul flower." When dropped, it floats like a butterfly, which is believed to be the way souls fly when they leave the body at death. Some say the soul looks like a butterfly, and the Tamang word for both (*bhla*) is the same. Because it is a seed, the Tamang see it as a fertility symbol. Condensed within its complex of meanings is its element of whiteness, another term for that which is "good." It represents good (white) as opposed to evil (black), life as opposed to death, growth as opposed to decay. In essence, it is an abstract concept symbolizing everything sacred and ideal in Tamang culture.

The psychological and existential transformation that occurs to the shaman during the intiation period has as its goal the establishment of the shamanic vocation. This is a cultural goal, one which is transmitted through traditional ways from guru to disciple. The cultural values represented in the *narling mendo* bcome important symbols of transformation during the liminal period of initiation; that is, they are symbols which through their inherent meaning impart cultural values to the individual, transforming the obligatory into the desireable, the undesired calling into a career.

Thus, the shaman becomes identified with the underlying principles of the white flower which is so conspicuous during all shamanic rituals. It is placed on the shaman's drum, stuck onto the rims of sacred vessels that contain offerings to the gods, affixed to the rice effigies of the gods that the shaman constructs to be the receptacles of the spirits during rituals. As mentioned before, *narling mendo* cover the *gufa* structure in profusion and are seen in the vision of the throne of Ghesar Gyalpo. In fact, the flower is a symbol of the Tamang shaman's "high god." It is this god that bestows curing powers on the shaman during the final initiation. The numinous positive ideas that are subsumed in the white flower convey the ideals and values of the society and serve as vehicles or guides for the reorganization of personality disrupted during the calling and other initiatory altered state experiences, by channeling sentiments into appropriate cultural pathways. This occurs at the dialectic moment when the anti-structure of "existential *communitas*" becomes transformed into a structure infused with the principles embodied in the sacred flower (see Turner 1969:129-133).

Now, although it is true that dominant symbols are preconscious, they carry their message directly to the unconscious, penetrating and altering the initiant's complexes. Levi-Strauss (1963:198-199) makes a distinction between the unconscious and the preconscious, seeing the latter as a "reservoir of recollections" amassed over a lifetime, and the former as empty of content by impinging structural laws upon everything that passes through it. I take another view, one more in line with dynamic psychology. While the preconscious may well be a reservoir of recollections, the unconscious is a reservoir of emotion and energy (see Freud 1961b:18-24). And, although the unconscious is probably structured (e.g., Jung's archetypes and Freud's Oedipus complex), its dynamism is also guided by the structure imposed by culture which becomes represented in dominant or key symbols. In this sense, the symbol is the *via regia* for the transformation of the individual.

The shaman's formal training ends with *gufa*. Now that the shaman has been through his initiatory affliction and has mastered it, the resulting controlled trance can be utilized in community context. He has been transformed; once afflicted and beset by chaos and confusion, his energies and motivations have been reorganized and redirected by the long initiatory process into a viable cultural vocation. The identification with the culturally valued ideals that transforms the individual, reintegrating him socially and psychologically, while similar in many respects to the methods and goals of contemporary Western psychotherapy, represents, however, an alternative to these systems. The reorganization of social role, motivations and world view (mazeway) of the shaman according to cultural ideology is a much more salient feature of shamanic initiation than are self-discovery, "individuation," introspective insight, or other personalistic psychological goals. Tamang shamanism is also distinct from yoga, with its goals of detachment, autonomy, and liberation from the world.

CHAPTER SEVEN

Psychotherapy in Tamang Society

The major social function of the shaman in Tamang society is the diagnosis and treatment of illness, physical and mental, as well as such personal problems as marital conflicts, economic difficulties and bad luck. The object of this chapter is two-fold: first I investigate the cultural context in which numerous physical symptoms, spirit possession and soul loss occurred in a specific case; then I examine the ritual performance and techniques used by the shaman in this case, comparing these to Western psychotherapy in order to account for their effectiveness. This one case is sufficient to illustrate a typical Tamang major healing ritual, not only because it contains three of the four categories of illnesses, but because all major healing *puja* are very similar, each having similar structure and purpose. Of course, there were some differences in the ways that my three primary informants performed major healing rituals, but these were of minor significance. One unusual feature of the ritual being described here is that the shaman conducting it is the brother of the patient, and he has been in conflict with her husband for some time. However, the fundamental aspects as well as the interpretation of the ritual are consistent with other rituals observed.

Numerous shamanic healing rituals were observed during fieldwork with the Tamang. I often accompanied Bhirendra and his disciples on their housecalls, where they would play the drum and sing the sacred stories, entering into trance and becoming possessed by a god or ancestor, or dispatching their souls from their bodies. All of this was done to dispel an attacking witch,

14. The shaman has fabricated this scapegoat
to lure attacking, illness-causing spirits away from his patient
by making them believe that a human sacrifice is being made to them.
The banana tree at the head is ascended in visions
by the shaman when he journeys to "other worlds."

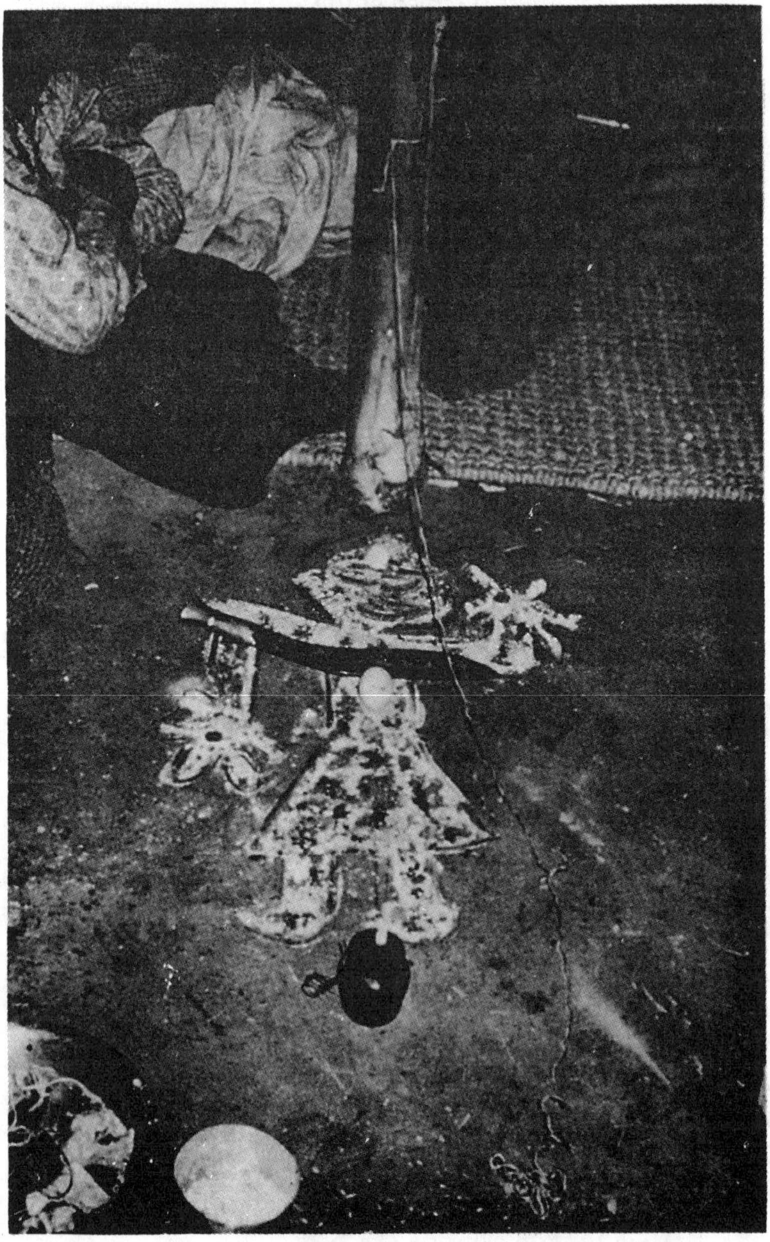

return a soul stolen by a spirit, or exorcise a possessing spirit, each a possible cause of illness. As mentioned previously, the etiology of the disorders treated by the shamans is always attributed to supernatural agents.

The rituals may be conveniently divided into two types: major and minor. The latter consists of reciting a spell or magical formula, and sometimes brushing away pain from the afflicted part of the body with a broom. These acts are often effective in themselves; however, if symptoms persist, then treatment escalates into a major healing *puja*. There were numerous recurrent cases requiring minor healing rituals, but during my year in the field there were no patients who received two major rituals. Of those patients for whom major rituals were performed, only three had previously had one. Nineteen major healing *puja* were observed in all. Twelve of these involved spirit possession. However, in only four cases did possession trance appear during the performance of the ritual, as it did in the case detailed below. In the others, possession of the patient was diagnosed as the cause of antisocial behavior, ranging from swearing at one's mother to attempted rape, and occurred prior to the *puja*. Consequently, the opportunity did not arise to observe the patients when they manifested their aberrant behavior. Of the four patients whose possession was observed in the rituals, three claimed in later interviews to have had complete remission of symptoms. In one case where symptoms continued, Bhirendra recommended the patient consult a doctor a few days after the *puja*. She was later successfully treated for swelling of the joints by the missionary doctors at Shanta Bhawan Hospital near Kathmandu. Bhirendra maintained that he appeased the spirits that had caused the illness, making it possible for the doctors to speed the patient's recovery from the physical symptoms "which would have disappeared anyway."

The ritual performance which will be described here is called *karga puja*,[1] and it is the most dynamic of all the major healing *puja*. *Karga puja* are always very dramatic and exciting ceremonies

[1] *Karga* means weapon and a *puja* of this nature would be considered

centering around the patient but also enlisting the involvement of the whole patrilocal extended family. Often there was evidence of an upset in the family equilibrium where two or more individuals were in conflict and one of them, the patient, became physically ill and possessed by a spirit. Thus, even organic symptoms appear to result from tension and anxiety.

For these reasons, I believe the shaman is most effective curing illnesses of a sociopsychological nature. The cure itself indicates this for it involves, as the following example demonstrates, the reorganization of sentiments within the family. Essentially, this chapter establishes, in agreement with Bourguignon's (1976b:12) argument, that "the indigenous definition of illness and the modification of the patient's position with regard both to the supernatural and to his position in society are directly relevant to cure." In other words, the curing activities involved in shamanic healing are not exercises in the treatment of organic disease but attempts at treating disturbing emotional states and interpersonal relations.

The Case History

The patient, Kanchi, is 42-years old. She is the youngest sibling in her family and has two elder brothers, Bhirendra being the oldest. Kanchi has been married to Mani for 14 years and has three children (a daughter, 16, from a previous marriage, and two sons, 9 and 12). Her marriage to Mani is monogamous; she left her first husband when he took a second wife. Kanchi, her parents and siblings, moved to Tin Chuli 28 years ago. Both of her marriages were arranged by her parents, although she knew both men before and consented to marry them after the families came to an agreement. Mani is her mother's sister's husband's

---

necessary if symptoms appear severe enough to cause death. However, it did not appear to me that the patients in any of the *karga puja* I observed were sick enough to die.

younger brother. To all appearances, Kanchi is a hardworking and devoted wife and mother.

Until one week before her *karga puja*, Kanchi seemed healthy and happy. She was often seated outside her house with her husband and children when I passed. Sometimes she would be rubbing mustard oil on Mani's back, as is commonly done in Nepal. She always waved and smiled as I passed, and one time even offered me a tall glass of fresh buffalo milk. All of Bhirendra's family was pleased with our working relationship. It brought him increased prestige in the community and probably even improved his credibility as a shaman. It certainly increased his income substantially, making it possible for him to provide a better standard of living for his family. Everyone in the family was kind to me and Kanchi was no exception.

One morning, I arrived at Bhirendra's house to find Kanchi on the front porch, having come for treatment for a headache and some eye problems. Bhirendra felt the pulse in each of her wrists for a few seconds, and diagnosed that Kanchi was being attacked by an evil spirit (*lagu*). For treatment, Bhirendra blew a *mantra* at Kanchi's head. This consisted of repeating the magical formula designed to dispatch the *lagu* and intermittently blowing on the afflicted area. Kanchi left immediately after the treatment, and walked briskly toward her house. She made no comment on the effectiveness of the ritual.

Several days later, Bhirendra told me that Kanchi's condition had worsened. Her vision was now blurred, she complained of back pains and could barely stand up. In all, her ability to maintain her normal household duties (cleaning, cooking, tending the animals and garden) was severely limited. She had lost substantial weight and was very weak. During another diagnostic session (at which I was not present), Bhirendra had told Kanchi that her planets were in a bad position because she was 42 (even-numbered years being unlucky) and this opened her up to attack. Thus the serpent-spirits (*nag*) were making her go blind and he feared that the "army of death" (Yama *dhut*) might take her life. Based on this diagnosis, he scheduled a *karga puja* to take place four days hence. *Puja* are generally performed on the night after a daytime diagnosis. However, in this case there was some confusion over where the *puja* was to be held, as the patient's house was very small, and it took four days to sort all the problems out.

Preparation consisted in purchasing and making ritual paraphernalia. For the offering to the gods, Bhirendra procured one egg, some rice beer, *raksi* (strong liquor made of grains or sometimes fruit), and cigarettes. The egg was to be offered to the gods, but the drinks and smokes were for the shaman and audience to consume during the ritual. A *pathi* (about 3½ kilos) of rice were also obtained. First this was cooked and then shaped into twelve images of the shamans' gods which were set up in a sacred area in front of where the shamans would perform the ritual. During the *puja*, the gods descend into these images, taking their seats there, and are used by the shaman to protect himself and the patient. *Narling mendo* flowers were placed on top of each of the rice figures.

The day before the *puja*, one of the villagers told me about a debt Bhirendra owed to his brother-in-law, Kanchi's husband, who was very angry with him. Mani had asked Bhirendra for the money, but Bhirendra refused saying that he was broke. By this time, Bhirendra had been working for me for six months and had been openly extravagant in his spending, running up large bar tabs, and patronizing the butcher's stall regularly. The villager who related this story was Mani's friend. He had come to me to ask whether I would consider garnishing the sum from Bhirendra's wages.

When Bhirendra was informed of this conversation, both he and his mother were visibly upset. They said Mani had approached Bhirendra a few days earlier, and was very angry when Bhirendra declined to repay the debt. Bhirendra explained to Mani that he had a big family to feed (mother, father, wife and four children), and that he couldn't afford to pay the debt off at this time. He further explained to me that he had borrowed the money to pay court expenses in a dispute over some land ownership with his former wife. He intended to repay the debt from the rice harvest off that piece of land, if he won the case as he expected. The rice would not be harvested for seven more months, however. Right now, he needed to buy some new clothes for his children, who had not had new garments for nearly a year. He motioned toward the children, muttering "rags, rags." His mother brusquely interjected that her son-in-law had more money than they and fewer mouths to feed. It was obvious I had entered into a family feud.

Tamang healing *puja* are customarily conducted in the house of the patient, with the patient's husband bearing the full cost of the ritual. At all of the rituals of this type which had been observed, the patient's husband was an active participant, giving complete support to his wife. Uncharacteristically, Mani refused to allow Bhirendra into his house, to attend the *puja*, or to pay for it. Angered at Bhirendra, Mani was retaliating by punishing his wife. By not paying for, or attending, her *karga puja*, he rejected her in a very graphic sense.

Kanchi was being forced to take sides in the dispute between her husband and her mother and brother. She was unwittingly in the middle of a heated family dispute, and was being forced to show her loyalty to one party or the other. Both choices were undesirable. Her aches, pains, weakness, blindness, etc., all appeared around the same time as the development of the family conflict, and it seems that this anxiety laden family situation may have been responsible for her physical symptoms.

The Ritual Performance

The *puja* took place at the home of the patient's husband's brother, who is also her mother's sister's husband. I was told that this larger, newer house was better suited to accommodate the large crowd that had assembled to watch the *puja*. But the day following the *puja*, Bhirendra admitted that Mani had been "acting stupid" and so another house had to be found. The house in which the ritual was performed was typically Tamang: a two-story and mud-finished frame covered with a thatched roof. The ritual was conducted on the lower floor, where the kitchen is and where the animals (chickens, goats, sometimes cattle) are kept. The family sleeps upstairs, on straw mats laid on the mud floor. As stated before, there is no electricity in Tin Chuli and so the rooms are very dark. On the night of Kanchi's *puja*, two small oil lamps provided all the illumination. Seto and Bhirendra sat against the short wall of the 10'x20' room, facing the audience. Bhirendra set up the rice statues before him, each in a specific space in the checkerboard-type sacred area. Before this area was placed one of the candles so that, while the rest of the room was nearly black, there was always a flickering of light upon the gods. The patient sat to the *bombo*'s right, next to the sacred area.

Bhirendra and his disciples began the *puja* by drumming and singing some of the important songs that relate the cosmogony, anthropogony and the tale of the separation of men and gods. The separation of men and gods story (Ta: *lha chabba me chabba*) provides a structure that outlines the performance of the *karga puja*. It sets forth the rules for its successful enactment.

Lha chabba me chabba describes how the gods took an ailing woman to heaven and, in exchange, gave man a goddess to wife. My informants explained that, in the beginning, gods and men lived together like men today, i.e., like neighbors who are members of exogamous clans. In order to heal the woman, the gods gave man the task of gathering together the ritual objects, among which were an egg, a fish, and a deer's leg. Angered at having to share his hunting catch with the gods and his goddess-wife, the man threw the deer's leg at his wife and broke her leg. This is why the gods took their daughter back and broke off relations with man, setting up curtains of various materials that act as barriers between the domains of heaven and earth. There is an important message for Tamang men in this tale, according to the informants. If one treats one's wife badly, she can by edict of the gods, so to speak, leave him. Also, a man is supposed to share what he has with his wife, and should care for her and not abuse her. In fact, this is essentially what a man promises his wife and her family during the marriage ceremony. Further, as the myth prescribes, the husband is supposed to provide all the necessary ritual articles.

Kanchi's *karga puja* lasted from 8:30 p.m. to 2:00 a.m. and, like all major healing rituals, was divided up into a number of dramatic acts. During the first two hours, the myths were sung. From time to time, Bhirendra stopped singing and playing the drum, and explained the meaning of each tale to the audience, which included Kanchi's parents, children, husband's brother's family, a few friends and neighbors, three *bombo* disciples, my field assistant, my wife and myself: 17 in all.

The second part of the ritual was the offering to the planet gods. A *mantra* was recited and some incense burned to please the gods' olfactory senses; rice was tossed into the air as a food offering. Bhirendra believes that the magical formula he whispers has the effect of a command; i.e., the recitation guarantees the gods' obedience. They have no choice but to obey, and the food keeps them happy. As mentioned previously, the shaman is the master of spirits.

Seto began the next act of the ritual by picking up his drum and beginning to play. His drumming was loud and rapid, quite different from the percussion during the myth recitations. As he played, Seto began to shake and then, gradually over a period of perhaps five minutes, his face began to change; his eyes glazed over and he stared, eyes half closed, into space. He straightened his back and suddenly, as if "hit" by a bolt of lightning, his body reverberated and the shaking became convulsive. His crossed legs beneath him bounced up and down, and his head bobbed. The drum beat grew markedly louder and lost its rhythm as the cadence was interrupted by two or three sharp beats at the moment of possession, followed by a few strokes that missed the drum altogether.

Seto slowed down, almost coming to a stop. Trembling only slightly, he began to speak. The spirit occupying his body was his tutelary spirit. It spoke, saying that Kanchi was being attacked, and that it would assist at her *karga puja*. Seto was hit again with convulsive movements as the spirit raged in his body. As he calmed down, it spoke again: an evil spirit had stolen Kanchi's soul. She had been frightened and her soul, which fled her body, had been captured. Kanchi agreed and told how she had spilled boiling water on herself and one of her children. She hadn't felt right since that time; her consciousness had been "flitting in and out."

Seto resumed the drum playing and began to shake again, but his tutelary guru no longer spoke. Suddenly, Kanchi began shaking; her tremors increased very rapidly until they became extremely hard and, at their highest pitch, she let out a blood-chilling scream. Bhirendra and Seto moved in on her, asking her questions. But she couldn't be reached and her trembling continued. The shaking grew harder and she was "hit" again. Her facial expression changed, she grew angry and then yelled at Bhirendra in a very loud voice quite unlike her normal tone. The voice told Bhirendra that he was no good, and that his *bombo* gods had no power. She spat at the sacred area and then lunged forward to knock down the gods' images.

Everyone was caught off guard by the attack, but Bhirendra and Seto reacted quickly enough to keep Kanchi from causing much damage. They restrained her against a wall and, when she fought back, Seto took off his rosary beads and struck her lightly but repeatedly around the neck. She slumped forward. Seto's blows were certainly not hard enough to hurt her. Rather, they scared and calmed her down. The threat he posed with the beads was spiritual, not physical. Raising the sacred rosary over his head was like calling into action the 108 gods the beads represent. It was similar to raising a cross in the presence of one possessed by the devil. She cried while she was being beaten, and each time Seto raised his arm over his head, his face set in exaggerated grimace, she winced and lifted her arm to protect herself. Kanchi, that is the spirit possessing her, was on the defensive. Seto had the situation under control.

Now Bhirendra and Seto again interrogated Kanchi. "Who are you?" they asked repeatedly. Seto leaned forward threateningly, rosary in hand. The spirit possessing Kanchi replied, identifying itself as a graveyard ghost. "Why have you come? Is it to cause trouble?" Seto asked. Kanchi began shivering again. Seto put his rosary around his neck and, picking up his drum, began to play again. The beat was rapid and now both Kanchi and Seto shook in unison. Bhirendra stood next to Kanchi, rosary in hand, and threatened the evil spirit with violence if it didn't leave at once.

The drumming increased in tempo and again Seto was hit. After some furious shaking, his movements decreased and the possessing spirit identified itself as the same spirit that had earlier possessed Kanchi. Seto took a handful of rice and tossed it over Kanchi and himself, dispatching the spirit. Kanchi's shaking ceased and she leaned against a wooden pillar, exhausted.

Bhirendra explained that Seto had transferred the spirit from Kanchi's body into his own, thereby exorcising it. Since Seto was protected by the gods he had called down during the first part of the *puja*, the evil spirit couldn't harm him. The *bombo* then recited a *mantra*, commanding some of the gods who had earlier taken their place within the sacred area to chase the graveyard spirit away. Seto had thrown rice[2] over himself and Kanchi in order to send the spirits back to their home. This cultural cue is always used to signal release from possession and the awakening of normal personality in both *bombo* and patient.

After the myth recitation early in the *puja*, there had been a beer and cigarette break. Now everyone took another break while Bhirendra finished preparing for the *puja*'s next act. He cleared an area on the floor and drew an effigy (Ta: *luey*) with blue, red and yellow ochres, white flour and black ground charcoal. A tall (5') banana tree was nailed into the mud floor at the *luey*'s head. He resumed his performance by picking up his drum, dancing as he beat it. The drum beats were hard but rhythmic, his steps short and quick. This particular *bombo* dance is intended to raise anger in the shaman's heart. Fierceness is required to deal with the "army of death," sometimes called *karga*, sometimes called Yama *dhut*.

While he was dancing, Bhirendra called on his familiar spirit helpers to surround his body and protect him before he opened the "heavenly doors" and sent his soul from his body to rescue Kanchi's soul from the land of death (see Figure 1). First he asked his *mukhiya guru* to possess him. This was signaled by his

[2] Because rice is white, it shares many of the qualities of goodness and purity attributed to the *narling mendo*, described in Chapter 6. It is also a holy food used to feed and thus stave off evil spirits.

shaking, which blended into the dance. The dance steps were still the same, but now he danced quicker, moving around the room to encircle Kanchi, the audience, the sacred area and the *luey* with his steps. The drumming became louder and faster, just as it always does before a *bombo* is possessed. Suddenly, Bhirendra fell to the ground, and lay immobile, drum resting on his chest.

During the cigarette break that divided this act from the next, Bhirendra explained that he had collapsed because his soul, which animates his body, had departed for Yama *lok*. It had climbed the banana tree[3] and seen, "as if in a dream," the flag of death erected for Kanchi in Yama *lok* by the Yama *dhut*. He had destroyed it and returned to his body. Pointing to the top leaves of the banana tree, Bhirendra confided that the Yama *dhut* were perched there. They had come down from Yama *lok* on his shoulders, and were now awaiting the sacrifice he had promised them.

When his explanation was finished, Bhirendra motioned to Seto and another disciple. They rose and moved the patient next to the *luey*. Winding five strings together, strings the same colors as those used in drawing the *luey*, they tied one end to the banana tree and the other around Kanchi's neck. They returned to their seats and had another cigarette before the next act began.

Thus far, the *puja* had gone through four acts. First, the *bombo* had sung the sacred stories. Secondly, they made an offering to the planet gods. In the third act, Seto called on his main god to enter his body and make a diagnosis. At the end of this segment, Kanchi became possessed, was interrogated and exorcised. The fourth act involved Bhirendra's magical flight.

The *puja*'s most dramatic act, the cutting of the *karga*, was next. The *bombo* began by singing a *kheba*[4] (Ta.). The song

[3] The banana tree conforms to the symbolism of the *axis mundi*, described in detail in Chapter 6 (see Eliade 1964:259ff).

[4] *Kheba* are songs the *bombo* employ to call on spirits and gods to enter the ritual area. Like *mantra*, *kheba* command the gods. *Kheba* were sung early in the *karga puja* when Bhirendra invited the gods of the sacred area to take their seats.

promised the Yama *dhut* a human sacrifice (the *luey* in disguise) in addition to the patient, and invited them to feast on the rice, beer, and liquor set around the *luey*. Bhirendra promised the Yama *dhut* an opportunity to copulate with 1,600 maidens he would provide. Motioning toward Kanchi, he asked the Yama *dhut* attacking her to join in the festivities; they had only to walk over the strings and be seated in the branches of the banana tree.

When he was convinced that the five Yama *dhut* had passed over into the top of the tree, Seto resumed his drumming. Bhirendra rose and danced. While dancing, he bent over and picked up a dagger which he whirled fiercely over his head, chopping at the ceiling and rafters. The dance grew faster and faster until the drumming shifted into hard, short, fast beats. At that moment, one of the assisting disciples killed a chicken and dribbled its blood all over the *luey*. Simultaneously, Bhirendra cut down the banana tree and severed the strings. Other members of the audience grabbed Kanchi's arms and briskley moved her over to the far side of the room.

Once the tree had been felled, the Yama *dhut* had no light and could not see. Since they are stupid, sense-dominated creatures, they rushed eagerly toward the smell of blood. Blinded and engrossed in their meal, they did not notice that Kanchi had been moved away and that the strings, the road back to her, had been severed. In this manner, the purpose of *karga puja* was fulfilled. The Yama *dhut* had been duped.

The sixth ritual act of the evening was the return of the patient's soul. In it, the spirit who had captured the frightened soul is forced to give it up. The returning of the soul is symbolized by placing a *narling mendo* (as mentioned earlier, known as a "soul flower") on Kanchi's forehead as blessing.

The last ritual act of the evening was an offering to Shabi Aama, the goddess believed to carry away all impurities and pollution. A candle was placed in a leaf-plate that contained her offerings, and the shaman said a *mantra*. The leaf-plate was carried out of the house and placed at the first crossroads.

The ritual was an excited stressful event, but once it was over, life returned to normal to the observable relief of everyone. For the moment, the Yama *dhut* had been defeated and the patient had been saved. Everyone, including Kanchi, laughed, drank and smoked, while a couple of the disciple shamans cleaned and cooked the chickens which would now serve as a holy meal for all assembled except the patient. It is not appropriate for the patient to partake in the meal since the chicken was sacrificed in her stead.

Psychotherapeutic Elements

The ritual for Kanchi, and many of the others witnessed in Boudha and Tin Chuli, were clearly cultural mechanisms for alleviating stressful social situations. They were precipitated by a breakdown in social relations. By alleviating these problems, the symptoms were relieved. Thus, it is necessary to understand the social context or idiom if the function of the shaman in Tamang curing rituals is to be understood.

Just as related in the myth that describes the curing ritual the gods ordered done for the goddess, the overwhelming majority of Tamang healing rituals are done for women.[5] I. M. Lewis (1966, 1971) suggests that, in some sexist societies, where women are denied access to political and religious careers and men monopolize the social structure,[6] implying the subordination and deprivation of women, a basic hostility develops between the sexes. The protest against this is expressed by women through the culturally sanctioned idiom of spirit possession. In essence, Lewis (1966: 315-316) maintains that, in the "war between the sexes," possession is used as an "oblique aggressive strategy." Most typically, the symptoms are used to manipulate the immediate social situation

[5] Similar situations have been observed in Africa. See Harris (1957), Lewis (1966, 1971), and Messing (1958).

[6] There is a myth related by the Tamang that explains why women do not have mustaches. This is because Guru Rinpoche's wife lied to him. It is generally felt that women are spiritually inferior to men. In fact, Tamang men believe that being born female is proof of bad *karma* in former lives. Bhirendra was uneasy and answered awkwardly when my wife questioned

of husband and wife (in the cases observed in Nepal, this agressive strategy did not appear to be consciously employed) so that, when a sufficient amount of anxiety is created, a woman has the means to compel her husband to do something to show he cares for her. Confirming Lewis's analysis, the Tamang husband who pays for and participates in an expensive *puja* for his wife's benefit is indeed showing his concern.

The question Lewis does not consider is why some women who face similar frustrating situations succumb to possession and others do not. Wife beating and other forms of maltreatment occur frequently among the Tamang. However, such behavior is not condoned; the men who gossip in the taverns and tea shops often discussed their own and others' wife abuse proclivities in a pejorative tone. And, of course, Tamang sexual biases apply equally to all women.

What Lewis calls an oblique aggressive strategy is called "a secondary gain from illness" by Freud (1953:382f). He (1953: 383) writes, "Consider the commonest example of this sort. A woman who is roughly treated and ruthlessly exploited by her husband will fairly regularly find a way out in neurosis . . . her illness now becomes a weapon in her battle with her dominating husband—a weapon which she can use for her defense and misuse for her revenge." Here Freud does not maintain that the ego wills and creates the neurosis, merely that the ego puts up with it and

---

him about this. Still he did not deny that he believed it to be so. Further, as mentioned earlier, women are denied religious participation: there are no female Tamang shamans and no nuns in the Tamang Buddhist religion (although Tamang women can leave their villages and enter Tibetan Buddhist monasteries if they wish). Women are financially deprived as well in that they cannot inherit their parents' wealth unless there are no male offspring, in which case control of the inheritance is given to the woman's husband. I know of one case where a woman tried, unsuccessfully, to sell her property after she and her husband were divorced. Polygyny further adds to the Tamang woman's general insecurity. If a woman has no male children, it will not be long before a new wife is taken into the family, and the old wife relegated to menial chores.

makes the best out of it. The neurosis is, according to Freud, primarily the result of unconscious conflict, repression and fixation of libido at early developmental levels.

Lewis (1971:200), however, attaches no real significance to this underlying psychopathological disposition with respect to possession states. J. and I. Hamer (1977:372) raise the same question in their account of spirit possession among the Sidamo of Ethiopia: why don't all deprived individuals become sick? They reach the conclusion that only those who have unsuccessfully attempted to overcome their dependency relationship with their parents succumb to possession. Rycroft (1968), a psychoanalyst, suggests that possession occurs only in those individuals who have a deep conviction of defeat and insignificance acquired in early childhood. Conversely, Mayou (1975:468) posits that the potential for hysterical (including possession phenomena) reactions is universal and may be elicited in any individual under the right set of stressful circumstances. He further maintains that much hysteria is accepted as normal and appropriate in any society, and only a small proportion is considered to be a form of illness. Hollender and Hirsch (1964:1072) argue that the greater the stress, the less need there is for an individual to be predisposed (by virtue of a weak ego) to hysterical reactions. In other words, an inverse relationship exists between stress and predisposition to hysteria.

It is reasonable to conclude that the stress threshold for hysterical behavior varies among individuals, and these differences may well reflect feelings of dependency, defeat and inferiority. We all have potential for such reaction when extreme stress occurs, but the greater part of the population is able to inhibit emotional hysterical reactions, at least within the limits considered normal by society, in coping with everyday stress. Thus only a small minority of potential "hysterics" are considered ill at any given time in any society. This confirms my field observations where many contributory factors comprised the distress of women in general, but very few cases of possession occurred. However, when possession was manifested, it served as an oblique aggressive strategy, i.e., it served secondary gain.

Even in these cases, family conflict was not necessarily confined to husband and wife, as suggested by Lewis. Numerous cases occurred where tensions existed between members of the same sex (see Wilson 1967:372). As might be expected in a patrilocal extended family, there were cases where conflict between a new wife and her husband's mother led to illness for which the *bombo* was consulted. Tensions also existed between co-wives. What seems significant is the stressful nature of the family situation, no matter which members are involved. Kanchi's case, however, follows Lewis's model.

According to Bhirendra and his mother, Kanchi had been mistreated by her husband. During the ritual, they said she had been beaten by him earlier (although I saw no bruises). They said that Mani had tried to physically throw Kanchi out of her house, but that she had refused to leave. Everyone present seemed to concur. However, Kanchi made no comment. Still she made no denial either. It seemed that Kanchi and Mani had had a terrible argument precipitated by the conflictual nature of the relationship between her brother and husband. Immediately following the flare-up in their relationship, Kanchi's symptoms appeared. If the two events, the outbreak of illness and the conflictual situation, are connected in a cause/effect relationship, as the evidence indicates, then Kanchi's illness was related to the psychogenic stress created by a deep-seated conflict of loyalties.

What could Kanchi do? Could she, like the goddess in the myth, return to her parents and renounce the man she married and the life she has made for herself? The mythical heroine, before being compelled to return, used numerous devices to prevent being taken away from her husband. For example, she tried to keep her husband awake all night playing cards, so that he could oppose her father when he arrived. By staying awake, her husband showed concern for her. However, in the myth he fell asleep and thus lost his wife. Kanchi's symptoms appear to be a means by which to arouse her husband's sympathy and get him to show that he cares for her. The fact that Kanchi stopped performing her normal household duties was additional protest. This is what Lewis (1971:32) means by "oblique aggressive strategy" functioning to resolve social conflict; i.e., an attempt to bring the parties together for a reconciliation.

The Tamang shaman follows his mythical charter. He calls for a ritual requiring the participation and support of the husband in order to cure his wife. So the *karga puja* is a cultural mechanism seemingly designed to alleviate two interrelated problems at the same time: it releases the patient from her psychosomatic symptoms and simultaneously restores the proper sentiments to what Radcliffe-Brown (1952) calls "the actually existing network of social relations."

However, in this instance, the strategy failed. Kanchi's husband refused his support. He did not sanction the *puja* which, in a sense, told Kanchi that he did not care for her and that she should leave. However, something very unusual occurred. Kanchi did not leave Mani's house. Rather, Mani's older brother interceded on her behalf, offering his house for her ritual. It appeared that Bhirendra had refused to take no for an answer. His sister, Kanchi, was ill, and the *puja* had to be performed or she might die. He later confided that he would have held the *puja* in his own home except that it was customary for it to take place in the house of a person of the same clan as the patient.[7] So Bhirendra took it upon himself to approach Mahendra, Mani's brother, who is also his mother's younger sister's husband, and his best friend. Bhirendra, his mother and her sister all prevailed on Mahendra until he reluctantly agreed to have the *puja*, stipulating, however, that Bhirendra would have to bear the entire financial responsibility, which he did.

At Kanchi's *karga puja*, like the others observed, the most apparent psychotherapeutic element was the patient's catharsis. Kanchi's spirit possession was a very emotional experience for her. During it, she vented her aggression and frustration against her brother, behavior which would have been unacceptable in any other context, providing an intense emotional discharge.

[7] In Tamang society, a woman gives up her patrilineal clan and becomes a member of her husband's clan when she marries.

This aggression was not directed against her husband, as would have been expected according to Lewis's hypothesis.

There were many techniques employed in these rituals to bring about cathartic reactions. For example, during one *karga puja*, just as the *karga* strings were being cut, Seto was attacked by the Yama *dhut* who realized they had been tricked into accepting chicken blood and a *luey* sacrifice instead of the human sacrifice they expected. The unseen spirits grabbed Seto and threw him to the ground, wrestled him back and forth, rolling with him from corner to corner around the room, even over the sacred area with its god images. Seto screamed and shouted while this was happening and the people in the audience later said that they had been afraid that the *dhut* would come after them if they vanquished Seto. The patient had also been frightened, believing that if Seto were killed, the messengers of death would be free to continue their attack on her. Thus this dramatic shock treatment created high levels of anxiety in the audience as well as in the patient. The relief when Seto prevailed was obvious. These ritual acts parallel almost exactly the witchcraft cures mentioned by Fox (1964:186) among the Cochiti, which he believes have a profound curative effect on the patient. He writes, "The patient is put through a terrifying experience, 'saved,' and his heart restored. His relief is so great that, in many psychosomatic cases, the ceremony suffices as a cure."

Flagellation with the rosary is another technique used by the shaman to elicit a high pitched emotional reaction from the patient. As mentioned earlier, it appeared that it was used the same way a Christian exorcist might use a cross. I saw this technique used twice before, to make a witch speak through a patient that it was possessing. During these rituals, the patients were shaking uncontrollably, but they said nothing. Bhirendra tried to force the possessing agent to speak by threatening and coaxing, but had no success. But when he took off his rosary and held it over the patient, in each case the patient began to cry and speak.

The type of behavior manifested by Kanchi while she was possessed is very similar to what Sargant (1973:12-13) describes as the "ultra-paradoxical phase" of emotional abreaction. When this happens, behavior patterns that were previously learned suddenly become their opposite. That is, things once loved and respected become loathed, as when Kanchi turned her aggression on the gods and shamans. This state is followed by "inhibitory collapse," which was also observed after Kanchi's possession when she rested, exhausted, against the wall. Sargant believes that, at this stage, the mind is particularly susceptible to suggestion and that things learned in this state are believed with such conviction as to be analogous to conversion experiences. Commenting on similar types of curing rituals, Leighton (Prince, Leighton & May 1968:1178) says, "It is as if the whole procedure brought about a situation in which the structure of the patient's personality becomes soft, and then, after the emotional crisis, resets in a new form."

Leaving aside the matter of suggestion for the moment, it is probable that these intense emotional experiences have a beneficial psychological function in themselves. Kiev (1972:42) believes that emotional catharsis, by allowing the patient to ventilate aggression and frustration, provides "a sense of renewal and an improved capacity for dealing with reality." Kanchi's possession and catharsis was certainly a crisis experience; it appeared from a state of confusion, anxiety and emotional distress. During the crisis, her feelings were expressed through the spirit, a culturally relevant means, communicating to her brother what she thought of him and the position in which he had placed her. Through the ceremony, she was enabled to break out of her frustrating impasse and alter her intolerable situation. The ceremony thus gave her a means to ventilate aggression which was projected onto a spirit, relieving her of the burden of guilt from having shown disrespect for the gods and her brother.

In Tamang healing rituals, many psychotherapeutic effects seem to result from the personal influence of the shaman over the patient (see Prince 1973). However, also involved are the influence of cultural expectations for disease, and the belief in the efficacy of the *puja* (see J. Frank 1973:103-105). Through these elements, the illness is placed within a conceptual framework. The patient's symptoms and all the mysterious and chaotic feelings of distress were organized and their causes identified by the shaman during diagnosis prior to and at the time of the *puja*. The psychiatrist, E. Fuller Torrey (1972:16), posits that this categorization or "naming process" is a "universal component of psychotherapy which is used by both witchdoctors and psychotherapists alike." Torrey (1972:16) insists that, just by naming the disease, there is immediate reduction in the patient's anxiety. This is because once the illness is put into a cultural frame, definite expectations are aroused in the patient and his family. They immediately identify with others who have been cured of similar things by the shaman. In other words, once the disease entity is known, there are definite prescriptions for dealing with it. It does not matter what the name is; it can be a spirit, a complex or a germ. Levi-Strauss (1963:195) also believes that shamans, like psychotherapists, provide a "language" by which the inexpressible is given expression and that this transition marks a favorable direction in the healing process. Further, Kluckhohn (1944:112) suggests that explanations of unfortunate events by providing personification (i.e., spirit and witch causative agents) make it possible to initiate action and thus reduce anxiety. Evans-Pritchard's (1976:18ff) theory that witchcraft beliefs function to stabilize social relations by providing "explanations" for unfortunate events also applies here. All of these theories have one thing in common: they state that the diagnostic process through which illness is identified makes a transformation from chaos to order in the eyes of the patient and those concerned for him, and that has therapeutic effectiveness.

Aside from providing a common vocabulary by which to name illness, and catharsis, there are other psychotherapeutic aspects in Tamang healing *puja*. I mentioned before that the myth of the separation of men and gods, which is known to most Tamang and sung at every curing ritual, sets a model for the ritual. The myth provides the symbolic structure of a psychotherapeutic system. As in other theories of psychotherapy, it lays down the rules, procedures and a vocabulary. In this sense, myth and rite have the same psychological relationship to each other as theory and practice do in contemporary psychology. Just as a Western patient's expectations are conditioned by the therapist's theories and a relatively standard set of notions regarding therapy, the Tamang patient's framework of meaning is provided by cultural myth.

There are other therapeutic aspects of the *puja* that are distinct from Western conceptions. During the collapse phase, for example, the shaman, instead of making direct verbal suggestions, may manipulate cultural symbols. Part of Kanchi's diagnosis was that she suffered from soul loss and, after her possessing spirit had been exorcised and she had abreacted, Bhirendra and Seto performed the ritual to return her soul to her body. At this time, Seto picked up a *narling mendo* and stuck it on her forehead in the manner of giving blessing, as a symbolic gesture of returning her soul.

Symbolic communications during ritual may be very abstract. Healing symbols, like the *narling mendo*, as Wallace (1966:137) observes, "refer to extensive and complex ideas of value, structure, and transformation" whose verbal statement would be difficult, complex and take considerable time. As detailed in Chapter 6, the meaning of dominant symbols is polyvalent and thus they communicate several messages simultaneously to different levels of consciousness.

Levi-Strauss (1963:195) points out the psychotherapeutic effectiveness of symbolic communication, saying that symbols and symbolic gestures penetrate directly to the patient's complexes in cases where the spoken word could not get beyond the patient's defenses. In this respect, the Tamang shamans' use of the *narling mendo* is instructive. As has been described, it represents many of the cultural values of goodness, sacredness and growth. It is called "soul flower" and placing it on the patient's forehead symbolically depicts the returning of a lost soul, a cause of illness. The Tamang believes that the soul that is stolen normally resides within the forehead between the eyes. Such a symbolic gesture qualifies as a language; through it the therapist/shaman, as Levi-Strauss (1963:196) writes, "holds a dialogue with the patient, not through the spoken word but in concrete actions, that is, *genuine rites* which penetrate the screen of consciousness and carry their message directly to the unconscious."

The healing effectiveness of this type of "symbolic bombardment" is also mentioned by Kennedy (1977:382-383) who writes, from his Nubian experience, that "the marshalling of these symbols in Zar ceremonies throws the weight of all positive Nubian traditional values on the side of the patient."

So far, it has been shown that dominant symbols, possessed of compacted messages (healing and otherwise), are manipulated by the shaman during the collapse phase that occurs in Tamang healing *puja*. Further, according to the investigators cited above, when communicated after abreaction, these messages can produce profound effects on individuals. Sargant (1973:12-13), for example, believes abreaction plays a significant role in brainwashing, religious conversion, as well as in psychotherapy. The underlying effect of these exercises in Tamang healing *puja* is to transmute the patient's symptoms and behavior into socially useful channels. By accomplishing this purpose, the symbol serves as a guide or vehicle for the reorganization of the emotions released during the traumatic abreactive experience. In other words, the shaman uses the *narling mendo* in healing rituals similarly to the way it is used during initiation; at times of altered states, when the mind is particularly susceptible to suggestion, the *narling mendo* influences "mazeway resynthesis."

In the last interviews held with Kanchi, she said she had no memory of her spirit possession or of what the spirit said through her. All she knew was that she felt better. She no longer was under attack by the Yama *dhut* and no longer felt her life to be in danger. As she spoke, she was sitting in front of her house with Mani by her side. He seemed very supportive of her at the time. They had obviously reconciled. While it seemed plausible that the *puja*, by eliciting powerful emotions, had brought about a psychological change in Kanchi, there was no obvious reason why her normal social relations with Mani had been reestablished.

Social Healing

The highly emotional experience aroused during *karga puja* is analogous to what psychologists term "cathartic experience." In Tamang society, it has the function of disrupting old cognitive maps, sentimental pathways and social relations, while the messages and symbols of the *puja* restructure these according to cultural values. As indicated above, there appeared to be a complete remission of Kanchi's physical symptoms. During the four months of field observation which remained, Bhirendra was not called upon again by Kanchi in his professional capacity. Her internal conflict appeared to have been resolved, as had her marital dilemma. Kanchi and Mani were very much together. The social situation, however, was not resolved. Conventional wisdom with respect to such situations dictates that the ritual works by resolving social conflict, accomplished by bringing the parties together (in this case getting Mani to show his concern for Kanchi). But Mani had refused to support the *puja*. Bhirendra never did repay his debt. Still, Kanchi was no longer in an untenable choice situation. Her husband and brother were no longer making competing demands on her. She had been forced to have the *puja* because of her symptoms, and the activities which occurred during it had a profound effect upon her psychologically as well as upon her interpersonal relations.

Later interviews with Mani revealed that he did indeed love his wife. So while Kanchi's initial strategy had failed to win Mani's support through her crisis, they resumed their normal relationship once the ritual was over. Kanchi also maintained her normal relationship with Bhirendra and her mother. Why did Mani accept Kanchi now? What changed his mind? He acted as if Kanchi herself had denounced Bhirendra, and not the spirit that possessed her. There must have been a suspension of belief in his wife's possession, even if this disbelief was only a hunch, an intuition that was unacceptable within the framework of cultural convention, but which nonetheless influenced his attitude. When questioned about this, Mani denied that it was Kanchi who had spoken, stating in agreement with her that it was the spirit that had spoken. His actions and his statements, however, seemed incongruous.

Of course, once Kanchi's symptoms subsided, she returned to her normal domestic role which, as mentioned earlier, included wifely duties like cooking and cleaning. It is possible that the change in her behavior affected Mani's previously quarrelsome disposition. However, it must be noted that the causes for his anger had not been alleviated.

It is also conceivable that, by paying for the ritual, Bhirendra in effect repaid Mani, but neither man acknowledged this. Rather, each expressed their animosity toward the other. Bhirendra did not pay for the ritual because he owed a debt to Mani but because Kanchi was his sister. It is possible, however, that Mani derived satisfaction from seeing Bhirendra pay for the *puja*, a responsibility normally belonging to the patient's husband.

Bhirendra denied that Kanchi would ever speak to him as she had on the night of the *karga puja*; she would never denounce the gods. He insisted that what had spoken was the jealous spirit. His sister loved him, and he her. "After all," he said, "I paid for the ritual." Still, he seemed too adamant. He never even allowed an opportunity for questioning. The morning after the ritual, he, Seto and two other friends surprised me with an early visit to my house. Unsolicited, he explained all these matters in a tone that communicated his determination to make his point. It was evident that morning that this was not Bhirendra's first such conversation that day. In fact, he spoke as if trying to convince the others along with himself. He repeatedly mentioned that Kanchi had been possessed the previous evening, and each time his friends nodded in agreement. I felt I was witnessing the establishment of consensus. What had occurred during the ritual was so unusual that even the ritual experts seemed momentarily shaken in their faith.

Bhirendra, like Mani, seemed ambivalent over the issue of Kanchi's possession. They behaved as though they simultaneously *believed* and *didn't believe* it. The cultural belief system dictated that they accept the possession explanation, but they both acted as if there was some disbelief underneath this. That is, the cultural explanation they offered to me and themselves was a means of rationalizing the situation for their own benefit; below this was something inexpressible, even unthinkable, that affected them deeply.

Kanchi said she remembered nothing, only that she believed she had been possessed. Thus everything she had said was projected on the heavens, freeing her of any guilt, and of course any reason for Bhirendra to be upset with her. She had neatly escaped the precarious situation of having to make a choice between two parties to whom she owed loyalty; now she no longer had to make a choice at all. She could maintain positive relationships with both camps, something which had seemed impossible before the *puja* was performed. She had been able to tell Bhirendra off and, at the same time, not tell him off. By denouncing him, she took her husband's side; by not denouncing him (i.e., by attributing the words to a spirit), she was able to retain relations with him and their mother.

What I have suggested here is that a social conflict between Mani and Bhirendra, as well as the conflicts which were precipitated by this between Mani and Kanchi, and between Bhirendra, his mother and Kanchi, led to the development of Kanchi's illness. The situation is illustrated in Figure 2:

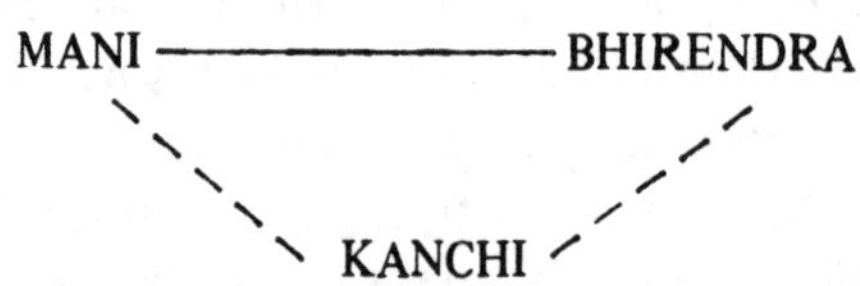

Figure 2

The hard line represents the conflict situation which was not resolved by the *puja*. The broken lines indicate those which were. The *puja* enabled Kanchi to express her unconscious feelings, a catharsis allowing her to feel secure regarding her true loyalties. Aspects of the belief system and their expression in the separation myth and *narling mendo* came into play in the *puja*, guiding the patient's sentiments into valued pathways of marriage and health, among other qualities. All of this took place on an unconscious level. The connection between the symptoms and what gave rise to them, i.e., the social conflict, was unknown to Kanchi.

Now whether or not the patient is completely cured, i.e., if the patient ever suffers from spirit possession or other symptoms again, does not seem to be important to the Tamang. The *puja* is not specific to "mental disorder" but is a cultural mechanism for solving social and psychological conflicts. Since these conflicts constantly arise in the life of all individuals, what is being treated by the Tamang shaman cannot be permanently cured. The Western psychotherapeutic ideal is to better prepare an individual to come to terms with his conflicts. We encourage independence through our therapies, using terms such as "self-realization," "individuation," and others to express this goal. The Tamang on the other hand, are not concerned with such preparations, but have devised a cultural mechanism to deal with conflicts whenever they arise.

The question remains whether the type of "cure" represented in the *karga puja* is as psychotherapeutically effective as therapy involving conscious insight into defenses. Kiev (1964:27) and Devereux (1956:18f) believe that "primitive" therapies provide only "social remissions" and "corrective emotional experiences," leaving the patient vulnerable, although such therapy is still valuable to both patient and community.

In the previous chapter, it was noted that, while the shaman does not achieve "insight" in the psychoanalytical sense, he does attain a "remembering," "repeating," and "working through" in his relationship with the guru. This is not the case in curing rituals. The patient does not remember the trance and, while the diagnosis may identify and explain symptoms, the patient has no memory of his possession-trance. Expression of problems and frustrations in the cathartic ritual are denied; there is no introspection into their meaning. Yet possession, which is an emotional catharsis, is a positive curative experience in itself.

Conscious insight into defenses, independence, and introspection may not be as important as once believed. Numerous scholars including Frank (1973:224), Kennedy (1974:1175, 1179), Prince (1973:310) and Scheff (1979:77) have maintained that understanding of psychological causes is not necessary for cure and that suggestion, faith, catharsis, and group support are sufficient for the mastery of most psychoneuroses.

The cultural goals of Tamang healing rituals are distinct from the goals of Western psychotherapy. Rather than fostering independence, the healing ritual helps to reintegrate the patient into the family unit, restoring previous social roles by redressing social conflicts. The goals of shamanic training are also distinct from those of the healing ritual. The latter does not lead to a change of social status and role; the patient's possession is culturally interpreted as distinct from the shaman's calling or "crazy possession" which is seen as evidence of a divine election. Each type of possession signals a cultural process with a different purpose: shamanic initiation leads to control of trance and the establishment of a relationship with the spirits, a therapy lasting a number of years; whereas the patient's exorcism is achieved in one dramatic night-long ritual.

Conclusion

Rituals of affliction or healing rituals are generally placed in a separate category from life-crisis rituals (Turner 1967c:7ff). This tends to mute the fact that, while rituals of affliction have different therapeutic purposes than initiation ceremonies, they are similar in structure in that they exhibit the same tripartite scheme of all rites of passage: separation, margin, and incorporation (van Gennep 1908).

Further, both types of rituals are reactions to upsetting "critical" situations in the life of an individual. Seigerest (1977: 389) was probably the first to draw attention to the special role and status of the afflicted person in society. He shows that disease strikes at the victim's social situation; "it breaks the rhythm of our existence sharply. Night comes and other men sleep. But sleep eludes the sick man. Mealtime arrives, but the stomach of the sick person refuses food altogether or makes strange demands at odd hours. The sick man, therefore, lives differently from the rest of society–from the healthy. In short, sickness isolates." This isolation corresponds to van Gennep's separation phase: the removal of the individual from his normal social status, role and functioning. During this separation/isolation, the person dies to society. As Seigerest (1977:390) puts it, "The sick man is dead to society even before his physical death."

Isolation is "betwixt and between" status and roles. In it, the person "passes" through an ambiguous position which has few or none of the characteristics of the normal structure of his social life. This marginal, or "liminal period" is, as Turner (1969: 95ff) has said, an "anti-structure." It is during this period that the crucial aspects of the healing *puja* are usually carried out. And, if abreaction and collapse are to occur, it is most likely it will be during this phase. Further, this is when the sacred and dominant symbols are manipulated and their associations aroused in the patient's mind. It is these associations, as established before, that serve as vehicles *molding* the patient's transition.

The third phase of the ritual of affliction is aggregation. Here the passage is consummated, and the individual's place once more becomes stable. He again has duties of a defined type and is expected to behave according to the cultural norms and ethical standards.

Although the ritual of affliction does not mark an actual change from one status to another, it does mark a reaggregation into one's previous status. It is still the same three-fold process of all life-crisis rituals; however, the movement is from person → patient → person. Instead of representing a change in status, the movement represents a passage from what Wilson (1967: 374f) calls "status ambiguity" back into one's former position in the social network.

Still, it may be thought that there are structural differences between rituals of affliction and rites of passage, namely that rites of passage mark a change from A→B→C (e.g., person→margin →shaman), while rituals of affliction ideally mark a change represented thus: A→B→A. Thus, structurally, it appears that there is really no transition involved. This depends, however, on how transition is defined. Is it necessarily restricted to social status? In Tamang initiation rites, from the time of *guru puja* (the second level of initiation) onward, the individual is considered to be a shaman. *Gufa* (the final initiatory grade) enhances prestige, as well as status and role, but it does not change status or role.

Needham (1967:611) has shown that there is a definite correlation between transition rites and the use of percussion instruments. Some of his finest examples come from shamanic performances. He says that percussion or "noise makers are associated with the formal passage from one status or condition to another." "Condition" is the key word here. Thus life-crisis rituals can be defined as passage from "one status *or* condition" to another. The changed condition, in both types of Tamang rituals, is a transition from a pure to an impure condition during the liminal period, back to a pure condition again in the third phase. The impure condition, in both instances, is characterized by the individual's possession by evil spirits and interpreted as illness.

In this way, rituals of affliction can be categorized as life-crisis rituals, every bit as much so as rites of passage like Bhirendra's *gufa* experience and calling. Bhirendra's condition was changed during the crisis-liminal period of both these events. During *gufa*, he received a vision of Ghesar Gyalpo who instructed him and gave him a special *mantra*. This was the outcome of entry into the unstructured or paradoxical realm of the cemetery where the living dead reside. At the time of entry into *gufa* and during his calling, Bhirendra's status became ambiguous: he was forced to confront the powers responsible for illness and death which had isolated him from the community and broken the rhythm of his former existence. Each of these experiences served to intensify community values for Bhirendra and thus changed his condition. Kanchi's condition was also changed through her *karga puja* which reorganized the sentiments within her social interrelations. Aggregation in both cases is marked by a change from impure to pure condition. The milk (white liquid) Bhirendra was given in heaven by Ghesar Gyalpo during *gufa* purified him. Likewise, the training exercises that lead to spirit mastery, the overcoming of "crazy possession" and the acquisition of the shamanic career are called "purification rites" (Ta: *silba puja*) by the Tamang. Similarly, Kanchi became healed or pure again by having the evil spirit exorcised from her. This pure condition was symbolized by the placement of the white *narling mendo* on her forehead as a blessing.

In the previous chapters, the psychotherapeutic relationship between shaman and patients was explained, as were the psychological intiation procedures the neophyte shaman experiences at the hand of his guru. Both were viewed as psychotherapeutic.

Nearly all the elements detailed in the former situation exist in the latter as well. Catharsis or abreaction is among the more important of these. And, just as catharsis through spirit possession is brought about in the major healing *puja*, so it is in each of the shaman's initiations. The shaman becomes possessed numerous times during purification rituals. It was demonstrated that the shaman becomes an expert at abreaction through repeated effort, supporting Levi-Strauss's (1977:454) definition that the shaman is a "professional abreactor." The patient, on the other hand, never does achieve control of the spirits; they are mastered on the patient's behalf by the shaman during exorcism.

Further, many of the symbols appearing in the major healing *puja* also appear in shamanic initiations where they fulfill the same function; i.e., they serve as vehicles for cultural values. As the patient's sentiments are guided into a new mazeway resynthesis by the *narling mendo*, so is the shaman's crisis experience (his calling) resolved by an intensification of values represented in the *narling mendo*, strengthening his role, status and ability as a shaman.

It was mentioned earlier that the sick person occupies an ambiguous position in society. In fact, this position was described using Turner's (1967a:93) terms, as a "betwixt and between" state of normal social roles characteristic of all rites of passage. Other observers who have interpreted curing rituals have provided similar correlations. For example, Prince (1964:103) writes of a Yoruba curing ritual as "clearly a *rite de passage* from the sick mode to the healthy mode." Precisely the same description has been used to portray the shaman's situation during certain phases of his initiation. Thus both phenomena are extremely similar in structure and function in that they not only involve the same three-fold structure, but are also clearly therapeutic. In both instances, crisis experiences are typical.

It is my hypothesis that, during these critical experiences, symbols compacted with meaning guide the individual's emotions into culturally prescribed channels. Particularly significant for the Tamang is the *narling mendo* flower which contains in its repertoire of meanings many of the cultural values and norms. These values point toward healing, health and good will toward one's fellows. The influence of the *narling mendo* helps create positive social relationships. In Kanchi's case, as in other curing rituals observed where social tensions were involved, it had the effect of creating positive feelings between family members. It also created positive social sentiments in the shaman's initiatory sickness. Through its influence, Bhirendra, like other Tamang shamans, had his positive feelings toward the group renewed.

Thus, in both curing rituals and shamanic initiations, sentiments are called on that enhance social solidarity, whether they be in a marriage or other family relationship or in a relationship between a man and his society. This hypothesis is very close to the functional theory sponsored by Durkheim (1915), in his monumental work, *The Elementary Forms of the Religious Life*, that rituals evoke emotions that enhance an individual's social sentiments and counter an individual's feelings of isolation from his fellow men.

In some respects, then, rituals of affliction are structurally and functionally similar to the rites of passage among Tamang shamans. Furthermore, both initiatory and healing rituals involve a possession by spirits which are similar psychological states. As mentioned, the "creative illness" or calling of the shaman, as experienced by Bhirendra, resembles the "acute schizophrenic" experiences described by Silverman (1967) as problem-solving processes which, if allowed to run their course under benign and supportive circumstances, produce a reintegrated functioning personality. I did not conduct a personality assessment of Bhirendra. It is possible that some of his behavior, particularly that involved in shamanism, could be considered abnormal according to psychiatric criteria. But he was not conceived of being abnormal by the Tamang; he was accepted and accorded social status for his experiences.

The uncontrolled possession experienced by patients falls within the category described in the literature as "culture-bound reactive syndromes" (Yap 1977:374) and the "hysterical psychosis" as defined by Hollender and Hirsch (1964:1066f) and Langness (1967:154f): transient or brief thought disorder caused by stress, receding as suddenly as it appeared leaving no residue and usually followed by amnesia.[1] The shaman's role in Tamang society is to treat such illness by resolving the stressful social interrelationships that cause them. During healing rituals, the patients (mostly women who are socially deprived) get an opportunity to express their true feelings without assuming the responsibility for their actions. Because the things said, and the behavior manifested during the possessed state are contrary to prescribed behavior, suppression or even repression occurs. Thus the aspect of memory which is so important in shamanic possession is absent in this type of possession-trance.

The shaman's possession has been described as being of the mythopoetic variety (Yap 1960:126-129). There is no repression here for the shaman identifies with an honored and respected ancestor, bearer of desirable cultural values, not an evil spirit representing antisocial tendencies. Thus the dissociation occurring in this possession state does not necessarily lead to amnesia. Both the shaman's and patient's possessions, however, result from personal crises; both appear to be problem-solving mechanisms; both are a type of "transient psychosis" (see Hollender and Hirsch 1964). Further, many of the symptoms interpreted by the Tamang as being indicative of initiatory sickness are found in the involuntary trances experienced by patients. Both involve typical olonistic behavior like anxiety attacks, convulsions, antisocial behavior; and patients suffering from soul loss are described as seeking isolation, even wandering in a semi-trance state in cemeteries.

The primary distinction between these types of experiences appears to be the socio-cultural context in which they occur. That is, it is cultural recognition that separates these categories, officially designating one group as potential shamans and the other as

[1] Langness (1976:59) has suggested that the fundamental distinction between "possession" and "hysterical psychosis" is that the former is voluntarily induced while the latter is an undesired state. Thus Langness's (1976: 61-62) examples of possession are of shamans. The uncontrolled possession experienced by the patient precisely fits all of Langness's criteria for the hysterical psychoses.

being in need of treatment and exorcism. In Tamang society, it is men who become shamans and women who are primarily beset with illness. The forms of illness appearing in men that fall within the typical cultural pattern of spirit possession and soul loss may be encouraged and interpreted as shamanic phenomena. Tamang shamans like Bhirendra, who come from families in which shamanism is "quasi-hereditary," would seem particularly encouraged to become shamans and have such experiences. The symptoms appearing in women, or those which are quite atypical or idiosyncratic in men, are discouraged and interpreted apprehensively as illnesses. The possession occurring to potential shamans lead to training and control of the state that originally beset them. That is, the shaman's behavior leads to positive social recognition while the same behavior in the potential patient is seen as threatening to the social order and calls for treatment. The former corresponds to Lewis's (1971:32-34) concept of politically "central possession cults" whereas the latter corresponds to "peripheral possession," aggressive strategies of the politically weak and socially deprived. Thus the shaman's possession and his other trance states are institutionalized and, after training, are conceived of by the Tamang as normal (or hypernormal) behavior while the patient's behavior is considered abnormal. Yet these possessions that occur to potential shamans as well as patients are structural and functional equivalents in that they mark critical periods in the life of individuals and elicit culturally patterned psychotherapeutic procedures that promote social solidarity and alter antisocial behavior. Further, both appear to be endogenous problem-solving processes leading to psychological change although they are interpreted differently by the Tamang and are guided along distinct cultural pathways toward distinct cultural solutions, primarily depending on sexual status and family background.

References

Ackerknecht, E.

1943 Psychopathology, Primitive Medicine and Primitive Culture. *Bulletin of the History of Medicine* 14:30-67.

Assagioli, R.

1976 *Psychosynthesis*. Harmondsworth, England: Penguin Books.

Bateson, G.

1961 Introduction. In *Perceval's Narrative*. Gregory Bateson, ed., pp. v-xxii. New York: William Morrow & Company, Inc.

Berndt, C. H.

1964 The Role of Native Doctors in Aboriginal Australia. In *Magic, Faith and Healing*. Ari Kiev, ed., pp. 264-282. New York: The Free Press.

Beyer, S.

1973 *The Cult of Tārā*. Berkeley: University of California Press.

Bharati, A.

1975 *The Tantric Tradition*. New York: Samuel Weiser, Inc.

Bista, D. G.

1967 *People of Nepal*. Kathmandu, Nepal: Ratna Pustak Bhandar.

Blacker, C.
1975 *The Catalpa Bow*. London: George Allen and Unwin.

Blustain, H.
1976 Levels of Medicine in a Central Nepali Village. *Contributions to Nepalese Studies: Journal of the Institute of Nepal and Asian Studies* (Kirtipur, Nepal: Tribhuvan University) 3:83-105.

Bogoras, W. G.
1930 The Shamanistic Call and the Period of Initiation in Northern Asia and Northern America, *Proceedings of the 23rd International Congress of Americanists* (1928), pp. 441-444. New York.

Bourguignon, E.
1965 The Self, the Behavioral Environment and the Theory of Spirit Possession. In *Context and Meaning in Cultural Anthropology*. M. E. Spiro, ed., pp. 39-60. New York: The Free Press.
1968 World Distribution and Patterns of Possession States. In *Trance and Possession States*. R. Prince, ed., pp. 3-34. Montreal: R. M. Bucke Memorial Society.
1976a *Possession*. San Francisco: Chandler and Sharp.
1976b The Effectiveness of Religious Healing Movements: A Review of Recent Literature. *Transcultural Psychiatric Research Review* XIII:5-21.

Boyer, L., B. Klopfer, F. B. Brawer, and H. Kawai
1964 Comparison of the Shamans and Pseudo-Shamans of the Apaches of the Mescalero Indian Reservation: A Rorschach Study. *Journal of Projective Techniques and Personality Development* 28:446-456.

Breuer, J. and S. Freud

1955 Studies on Hysteria. In *The Standard Edition of the Complete Psychological Works of Sigmund Freud*. J. Strachey, transl. London: The Hogarth Press.

Bugental, J.

1965 The Existential Crisis in Intensive Psychotherapy. *Psychotherapy* II:16-20.

Campbell, J.

1959 *The Masks of God: Primitive Mythology*. Harmondsworth, England: Penguin Books.

Carstairs, G. M.

1969 Changing Perception of Neurotic Illness. In *Mental Health Research in Asia and the Pacific*. W. Caudill and T. Lin, eds. Honolulu: East-West Center Press.

Carstairs, G. M. and R. L. Kapur

1976 *The Great Universe of Kota: Stress, Change and Mental Disorder in an Indian Village*. Berkeley: University of California Press.

Casanowicz, I. M.

1924 *Shamanism of the Natives of Siberia*. Washington: Annual Report of the Smithsonian Institution.

Charcot, J.

1889 *Clinical Lectures on the Diseases of the Nervous System*. G. Sigerson, transl. London: New Sydenham Society.

Crapanzano, V.

1977 Introduction. In *Case Studies in Spirit Possession*. V. Crapanzano and V. Garrison, eds., pp. 1-40. New York: John Wiley & Sons.

Czaplicka, M. A.
1914 *Aboriginal Siberia*. Oxford: Clarendon Press.

David-Neel, A.
1959 *The Superhuman Life of Gesar of Ling*. London: George Allen and Unwin.

Desoille, R.
1966 *The Directed Daydream: A Series of Three Lectures Given at the Sorbonne* (January 1965). F. Haronian, transl. New York: Psychosynthesis Research Foundation.

Devereux, G.
1956 Normal and Abnormal: The Key Problem of Psychiatric Anthropology. In *Some Uses of Anthropology: Theoretical and Applied*. J. B. Casagrande and T. Gladwin, eds., pp. 23-48. Washington, D.C.: Anthropological Society of Washington.
1961 *Mohave Ethnopsychiatry and Suicide: The Psychiatric Knowledge and the Psychic Disturbances of an Indian Tribe*. Bulletin 175. Washington, D.C.: Smithsonian Institution Bureau of American Ethnology.

Douglas, M.
1972 Pollution. In *Reader in Comparative Religion: An Anthropological Approach*, Third Edition. W. A. Lessa and E. Z. Vogt, eds., pp. 196-202. New York: Harper & Row, Publishers.

Durkheim, E.
1915 *The Elementary Forms of the Religious Life*. J. W. Swain, transl. New York: The Free Press.

Eliade, M.
1958a *Yoga: Immortality and Freedom*. W. R. Trask, transl. Princeton, N.J.: Bollingen Foundation.

1958b *Rites and Symbols of Initiation*. W. R. Trask, transl. New York: Harper & Row, Publishers.

1964 *Shamanism: Archaic Techniques of Ecstasy*. W. R. Trask, transl. Princeton, N.J.: Bollingen Foundation.

1969 *Patanjali and Yoga*. C. L. Markmann, transl. New York: Schocken Books.

Elkin, A. P.

1977 *Aboriginal Men of High Degree*. New York: St. Martin's Press.

Ellenberger, H.

1964 La Notion de Maladie Créatrice. *Dialogue, Canadian Philosophical Review* III:25-41.

1970 *The Discovery of the Unconscious*. New York: Basic Books, Inc.

English, H. B. and A. C. English

1958 *A Comprehensive Dictionary of Psychological and Psychoanalytical Terms*. New York: David McKay Company, Inc.

Evans-Pritchard, E. E.

1976 *Witchcraft, Oracles, and Magic Among the Azande* (abridged). Oxford: Clarendon Press.

Evans-Wentz, W. Y.

1958 *Tibetan Yoga and Secret Doctrines*. W. Y. Evans-Wentz, ed. London and New York: Oxford University Press.

Fabrega, H. and D. Silver

1970 Some Social and Psychological Properties of Zinacanteco Shamans. *Behavioral Science* 15:471-486.

Fingarette, H.

1963 *The Self in Transformation: Psychoanalysis, Philosophy, and the Life of the Spirit.* New York: Basic Books, Inc.

Firth, R.

1959 Problem and Assumption in an Anthropological Study of Religion. *Journal of the Royal Anthropological Institute of Great Britain and Ireland* 89:129-148.

1964 Shamanism. In *A Dictionary of the Social Sciences.* J. Gould and W. Kolb, eds., pp. 638-639. New York: Free Press of Glencoe.

1967a Ritual and Drama in Malay Spirit Mediumship. *Comparative Studies in Society and History* 2:190-207.

1967b Individual Fantasy and Social Norms: Seances with Spirit Mediums. In *Tikopia Ritual and Belief.* R. Firth, ed., pp. 293-329. Boston: Beacon Press.

Fischer, R.

1972 On Creative, Psychotic and Ecstatic States. In *The Highest State of Consciousness.* J. White, ed., pp. 175-194. Garden City, N.Y.: Doubleday & Company.

Forer, B.

1963 The Therapeutic Value of Crisis. *Psychological Report* 13:275-281.

Foster, G.

1976 Disease Etiologies in Nonwestern Medical Systems. *American Anthropologist* 78:773-782.

1978 Medical Anthropology and International Health Planning. In *Health and the Human Condition: Perspective on Medical Anthropology.* M. H. Logan and E. E. Hunt, eds., pp. 301-313. North Scituate, Mass.: Duxbury Press.

Fox, J. R.

1964 Witchcraft and Clanship in Cochiti Therapy. In *Magic, Faith and Healing*. A. Kiev, ed., pp. 174-202. New York: The Free Press.

Fox, O.

1962 *Astral Projection: A Record of Out-of-the-Body Experiences*. Secaucus, N.J.: The Citadel Press.

Frank, J.

1973 *Persuasion and Healing*, Revised Edition. Baltimore: Johns Hopkins University Press.

Frank, W.

1974 Attempt at an Ethno-Demography of Middle Nepal. In *Contributions to the Anthropology of Nepal*. C. von Fürer-Haimendorf, ed., pp. 85-97. Warminster, England: Aris & Phillips Ltd.

Freud, S.

1953 (1916-1917) Introductory Lectures on Psycho-Analysis, Part III *The Standard Edition of the Complete Psychological Works of Sigmund Freud*, Vol. XVI. J. Strachey, transl. London: Hogarth Press.

1958a (1911) Psycho-Analytic Notes on an Autobiographical Account of a Case of Paranoia. In *The Standard Edition of the Complete Psychological Works of Sigmund Freud*, Vol. XII. J. Strachey, transl., pp. 3-84. London: Hogarth Press.

1958b (1914) Remembering, Repeating and Working-Through (Further Recommendations on the Technique of Psycho-Analysis II). In *The Standard Edition of the Complete Psychological Works of Sigmund Freud*, Vol. XII. J. Strachey, transl., pp. 145-156. London: The Hogarth Press.

1961a (1924) A Short Account of Psycho-Analysis. In *The Standard Edition of the Complete Psychological Works of Sigmund Freud*, Vol. XIX. J. Strachey, transl., pp. 191-209. London: The Hogarth Press.

1961b (1923) The Ego and the Id. In *The Standard Edition of the Complete Psychological Works of Sigmund Freud*, Vol. XIX. J. Strachey, transl., pp. 12-66. London: The Hogarth Press.

Fürer-Haimendorf, C. von

1956 Ethnographic Notes on the Tamangs of Nepal. *Eastern Anthropologist* 9:166-177.

1978 Unity and Diversity in the Chetri Caste of Nepal. In *Caste and Kin in Nepal, India and Ceylon: Anthropological Studies in Hindu-Buddhist contact Zones*. C. von Fürer-Haimendorf, ed., pp. 11-67. New Delhi: Sterling Publishers Pvt. Ltd.

Furst, P. T.

1972 Introduction. In *Flesh of the Gods; The Ritual Use of Hallucinogens*. P. T. Furst, ed., pp. vii-xvi. New York: Praeger Publishers.

1974 The Roots and Continuities of Shamanism. *Arts Canada* 184(84):33-60.

1976 *Hallucinogens and Culture*. San Francisco: Chandler & Sharp.

Gaige, F. H.

1975 *Regionalism and National Unity in Nepal*. Delhi: Vikas Publishing Pvt. Ltd.

Gillin, J.

1948 Magical Fright. *Psychiatry* 11:387-400.

Goldschmidt, W.

1959 *Man's Way, A Preface to the Understanding of Human Society*. New York: Holt, Rinehart and Winston.

Gould, H. A.
1957 The Implications of Technological Change for Folk and Scientific Medicine. *American Anthropologist* LIX:507-516.

Govinda, A.
1960 *Foundations of Tibetan Mysticism*. New York: Samuel Weiser, Inc.

Green, C. E.
1968 Lucid Dreams. *Proceedings of the Institute of Psychophysical Research*, Oxford University, Vol. I. London: Hamish Hamilton.

Hagan, T.
1961 *The Kingdom in the Himalayas*. New Delhi: Oxford and IBH.

Halifax, J.
1979 *Shamanic Voices: A Survey of Visionary Narratives*. New York: E. P. Dutton.

Hamer, J. and I. Hamer
1977 Spirit Possession and Its Sociopsychological Implications Among the Sidamo of Southwest Ethiopia. In *Culture, Disease and Healing*. D. Landy, ed., pp. 367-374. New York: Macmillan Publishing Co., Inc.

Hamilton, F.
1819 *An Account of the Kingdom of Nepal and of the Territories Annexed to this Dominion by the House of Gorkha*. Kathmandu: Ratna Pustak Bhandar.

Handleman, D.
1967 The Development of the Washo Shaman. *Ethnology* 6:444-464.

Harner, M. J.
1973 *Hallucinogens and Shamanism*. London: Oxford University Press.

Harris, G.
1957 Possession "Hysteria" in a Kenya Tribe. *American Anthropologist* LIX:1046-1066.

Hasrat, B. J.
1970 *History of Nepal*. Punjab, India: published by author and printed at V. V. Research Institute Press.

Heusch, L. de
1962 Cultes de Possession et Religions Initiatiques de Salut en Afrique. *Annales du Centre d'Etudes des Religions*. Brussels: Université Libre de Bruxelles, Institut de Sociologie.

Hilgard, E. R.
1978 *Divided Consciousness: Multiple Controls in Human Thought and Action*. New York: John Wiley & Sons.

Hitchcock, J. T.
1968 Nepalese Shamanism and the Classic Inner Asian Tradition. *History of Religions* 7(2):149-158.

Höfer, A.
1969 Preliminary Report on a Field Research in a Western Tamang Group, Nepal. *Bulletin of the International Committee for Urgent Anthropological and Ethnological Research*, Vienna 11:17-31.
1974 Is the *Bombo* an Ecstatic? Some Ritual Techniques of Tamang Shamanism. In *Contributions to the Anthropology of Nepal*. C. von Fürer-Haimendorf, ed., pp. 168-182. Warminster, England: Aris & Phillips Ltd.

Hoffman, H.

1961 *The Religions of Tibet*. E. Fitzgerald, transl. London: George Allen and Unwin Ltd.

Hollender, N. H. and S. H. Hirsch

1964 Hysterical Psychosis. *American Journal of Psychiatry* 120:1066-1074.

Howells, W.

1949 *The Heathens: Primitive Man and His Religions*. London: V. Gollancz.

Janet, P.

1907 *The Major Symptoms of Hysteria*. New York: Macmillan Company.

Jelek, W. G.

1974 *Salish Indian Mental Health and Culture Change: Psychohygenic and Therapeutic Aspects of the Guardian Spirit Ceremonial*. Toronto: Holt, Rinehart and Winston of Canada, Ltd.

Jochelson, W. I.

1908 The Koryak. *Report of the Jessup Expedition 1900-1901*, Vol. 10(2). New York: Memoirs of the American Museum of Natural History.

Jones, R. L.

1968 Shamanism in South Asia: A Preliminary Survey. *History of Religions* 7:330-346.

Jules-Rosette, B.

1975 *African Apostles: Ritual and Conversion in the Church of John Maranke*. Ithaca: Cornell University Press.

1976 The Conversion Experience. *Journal of Religion in Africa* 7:132-164.

1978 The Veil of Objectivity: Prophecy, Divination, and Social Inquiry. *American Anthropologist* 80(3):549-570.

Jung, C. G.

1953 Two Essays on Analytical Psychology. In *The Collected Works of C. G. Jung*, Vol. 7. R.F.C. Hull, transl. Sir Read, M. Fordham, G. Adler and W. McGuire, eds. Princeton, N.J.: Bollingen Foundation.

1954 Analytical Psychology and Education. In *The Collected Works of C. G. Jung*, Vol. 17. R.F.C. Hull, transl. Sir H. Read, M. Fordham, G. Adler and W. McGuire, eds. Princeton, N.J.: Bollingen Foundation.

1960 Recent Thoughts on Schizophrenia. In *The Collected Works of C. G. Jung*, Vol. 3. R.F.C. Hull, transl. Sir H. Read, M. Fordham, G. Adler and W. McGuire, eds. Princeton, N.J.: Bollingen Foundation.

1961 *Memories, Dreams and Reflections*. R. Winston and C. Winston, transl., Aniela Jaffe, ed. New York: Random House.

1962 Commentary on the Secret of the Golden Flower. In *The Secret of the Golden Flower*. R. Wilhelm, transl., pp. 81-137. N.Y.: Harcourt, Brace & World Inc.

1969a On The Nature of Dreams. In *The Collected Works of C. G. Jung*, Vol. 8. R.F.C. Hull, transl. Sir H. Read, M. Fordham, G. Adler and W. McGuire, eds. Princeton, N.J.: Bollingen Foundation.

1969b The Psychòlogical Foundations of Belief in Spirits. In *The Collected Works of C. G. Jung*, Vol. 8. R.F.C. Hull, transl. Sir H. Read, M. Fordham, G. Adler and W. McGuire, eds., pp. 301-318. Princeton, N.J.: Bollingen Foundation.

1969c The Transcendent Function. In *The Collected Works of C. G. Jung*, Vol. 8. R.F.C. Hull, transl. Sir H. Read, M. Fordham, G. Adler and W. McGuire, eds., pp. 67-91. Princeton, N.J.: Bollingen Foundation.

Junker, B. H.

1960 *Fieldwork: An Introduction to the Social Sciences.* Chicago: University of Chicago Press.

Kennedy, J. G.

1974 Cultural Psychiatry. In *Handbook of Social and Cultural Anthropology*. J. J. Honigmann, ed., pp. 1119-1198. Chicago: Rand McNally College Publishers.

1977 Nubian Zar Ceremonies as Psychotherapy. In *Culture, Disease and Healing: Studies in Medical Anthropology*. D. Landy, ed., pp. 375-384. New York: Macmillan Publishing Co., Inc.

Kiev, A.

1964 The Study of Folk Psychiatry. In *Magic, Faith and Healing*. A. Kiev, ed., pp. 3-35. New York: The Free Press.

1972 *Transcultural Psychiatry*. New York: The Free Press.

Kluckhohn, C.

1944 *Navaho Witchcraft*. Boston: Beacon Press.

Krader, L.

1967 Buryat Religion and Society. In *Gods and Rituals*. J. Middleton, ed., pp. 103-132. Garden City, N.Y.: The Natural History Press.

Kretchmer, W.

1969 Meditative Techniques in Psychotherapy. In *Altered States of Consciousness*. C. T. Tart, ed., pp. 219-228. New York: John Wiley & Sons, Inc.

Krippner, S.

1972 Altered States of Consciousness. In *The Highest State of Consciousness*. J. White, ed., pp. 1-5. Garden City, N.Y.: Doubleday & Company.

Kris, E.

1952 *Psychoanalytic Explorations in Art*. New York: International Universities Press.

Krishna, G.

1971 *Kundalini: The Evolutionary Energy in Man*. Berkeley: Shambala Press.

Labarre, W.

1972a *The Ghost Dance: The Origins of Religion*. New York: Dell Publishing Co., Inc.

1972b Hallucinogens and the Shamanic Origins of Religion. In *Flesh of the Gods: The Ritual Use of Hallucinogens*. P. Furst, ed., pp. 261-278. New York: Praeger Publishers.

Lambo, T. A.

1964 Patterns of Psychiatric Care in Developing African Countries. In *Magic, Faith and Healing*. A. Kiev, ed., pp. 443-453. New York: The Free Press.

Landon, P.

1928 *Nepal*, Volumes 1 and 2. Kathmandu, Nepal: Ratna Pustak Bhandar.

Landy, D.

1974 Role Adaptation: Traditional Curers Under the Impact of Western Medicine. *American Ethnologist* 2:103-127.

Langness, L. L.

1967 Hysterical Psychosis: The Cross-Cultural Evidence. *American Journal of Psychiatry* 124:2.

1976 Hysterical Psychoses and Possessions. In *Culture-Bound Syndromes, Ethnopsychiatry and Alternate Therapies*. W. P. Lebra, ed., pp. 56-67. Honolulu: University of Hawaii Press.

Lantis, M.

1960 *Eskimo Childhood and Interpersonal Relationship*. Seattle: University of Washington Press.

Laski, M.

1961 *Ecstasy*. New York: Greenwood Press.

Lederer, W.

1973 Primitive Psychotherapy. In *Religious Systems and Psychotherapy*. R. H. Cox, ed., pp. 236-253. Springfield, Ill.: Charles C. Thomas.

Lee, R. B.

1968 The Sociology of the 'Kung Bushman Trance Performance. In *Trance and Possession States*. R. Prince, ed., pp. 35-56. Montreal: R. M. Bucke Memorial Society.

Legend of the Great Stupa. K. Dowman, trans. Berkeley: Tibetan Nyingma Meditation Center (1973).

Leuner, H.

1969 Guided Affective Therapy: A Method of Intensive Therapy. *American Journal of Psychotherapy* 23(1):4-22.

Levi-Strauss, C.

1963 The Effectiveness of Symbols. In *Structural Anthropology*. C. Levi-Strauss, ed., pp. 181-201. New York: Basic Books.

1977 The Sorcerer and His Magic. In *Culture, Disease and Healing*. D. Landy, ed., pp. 445-453. New York: Macmillan.

Lewis, I. M.

1966 Spirit Possession and Deprivation Cults. *Man* I(3): 307-329.

1971 *Ecstatic Religion*. Harmondsworth, England: Penguin Books.

Li An-Che

1948 Bon: The Magico-Religious Belief of the Tibetan-Speaking Peoples. *Southwestern Journal of Anthropology* IV(1):31-41.

Loeb, E. M.

1929 Shaman and Seer. *American Anthropologist* 31:68-84.

Lommel, A.

1967 *Shamanism: The Beginnings of Art*. New York: McGraw-Hill.

Lot-Falck, E.

1970 Psychopathes et chamans yakoutes. In *Echanges et Communications. Mélanges Offerts à Claude Lévi-Strauss pour son 60e Anniversaire*. J. Pouillon and P. Marando, eds., pp. 115-129. The Hague: Mouton.

Lowie, R. H.

1965 Shamans and Priests Among the Plains Indians. In *Reader in Comparative Religion*, Second Edition. W. A. Lessa and E. Z. Vogt, eds., pp. 452-454. New York: Harper & Row.

Ludwig, A. M.

1969 Altered States of Consciousness. In *Altered States of Consciousness*. C. T. Tart, ed., pp. 9-22. New York: John Wiley & Sons, Inc.

Macdonald, A. W.

1975a The Tamang as Seen by One of Themselves. In *Essays on the Ethnology of Nepal and South Asia*. A. W. Macdonald, ed., pp. 129-167. Kathmandu, Nepal: Ratna Pustak Bhandar.

1975b The Healer in the Nepalese World. In *Essays on the Ethnology of Nepal and South Asia*. A. W. Macdonald, ed., pp. 113-128. Kathmandu, Nepal: Ratna Pustak Bhandar.

1976a Preliminary Notes on Some *Jhankri* of the Muglan. In *Spirit Possession in the Nepal Himalayas*, J. Hitchcock and R. Jones, eds., pp. 309-341. New Delhi: Vikas Publishing Pvt. Ltd.

1976b Sorcery in the Nepalese Code of 1853. In *Spirit Possession in the Nepal Himalayas*, J. Hitchcock and R. Jones, eds., pp. 376-384. New Delhi: Vikas Publishing Pvt. Ltd.

Maddox, J. L.

1923 *The Medicine Man: A Sociological Study of the Character and Evolution of Shamanism*. New York: Macmillan Publishing Co.

Malefijt, A. de Waal

1968 *Religion and Culture: An Introduction to Anthropology of Religion*. New York: Macmillan Company.

Malinowski, B.

1926 *Myth in Primitive Society*. New York: Norton Publishers.

Maquet, J.

1975 Meditation in Contemporary Sri Lanka: Idea and Practice. *Journal of Transpersonal Psychology* 7(2):182-195.

1978 Castaneda: Warrior or Scholar? *American Anthropologist* 80(2):362-363.

1980 Bhāvanā in Contemporary Sri Lanka: The Idea and Practice. In *Buddhist Studies in Honour of Walpola Rahula*. S. Balasooriya, et al., eds., pp. 139-153. London: Gordon Fraser.

Marmor, J.

1962 Psychoanalytic Therapy as an Educational Process. In *Science and Psychoanalysis*, Vol. 5. J. H. Masserman, ed., 289-290. New York: Grune & Stratton.

Maslow, A. H.

1971 *The Farther Reaches of Human Nature*. New York: Viking Press.

Mayou, R.

1975 The Social Setting of Hysteria. *British Journal of Psychiatry* 127:466-469.

Mehan, H. and H. Wood

1975 *The Reality of Ethnomethodology*. New York: John Wiley & Sons.

Messing, S. D.

1958 Group Therapy and Social Status in the Zar Cult of Ethiopia. *American Anthropologist* LX(6): 1120-1126.

Mironov, N. D. and S. M. Shirokogoroff

1924 Śramaṇa Shaman: Etymology of the Word "Shaman." *Journal of the Royal Asiatic Society*. North-China Branch (Shanghai) LV:105-130.

Moerman, D. E.

1979 Anthropology of Symbolic Healing. *Current Anthropology* 20(1):59-80.

Murdock, G. P.

1965 Tenino Shamanism. *Ethnology* 4:165-171.

Murphy, J. M.

1964 Psychotherapeutic Aspects of Shamanism on St. Lawrence Island, Alaska. In *Magic, Faith and Healing*. A. Kiev, ed., pp. 53-83. New York: The Free Press.

Myerhoff, B. G.

1974 *Peyote Hunt: Sacred Journey of the Huichol Indians*. Ithaca: Cornell University Press.

Myers, F. W. H.

1887 Automatic Writing – III, *Proceedings of the Society for Psychical Research*, Vol. 4, Part 11., pp. 241-242.

Nadel, S.

1965 A Study of Shamanism in the Nuba Hills. In *Reader in Comparative Religion*. W. A. Lessa and E. Z. Vogt, eds., pp. 464-479. New York: Harper & Row.

Naranjo, C.

1971 Meditation: Its Spirit and Techniques. In *On the Psychology of Meditation*. C. Naranjo and R. Ornstein, eds., pp. 3-132. New York: The Viking Press.

Needham, R.

1967 Percussion and Transition. *Man* 2(4):606-614.

Neher, A.

1961 Auditory Driving Observed with Scalp Electrodes in Normal Subjects. *Electroencephalography and Clinical Neurophysiology* 13:449-451.

1962 A Physiological Explanation of Unusual Behavior in Ceremonies Involving Drums. *Human Biology* 34:151-160.

Northey, W. B. and C. J. Morris
1974 *The Gurkhas*. Delhi: Cosmo.

Obeyesekere, G.
1969 The Ritual Drama of the *Sanni* Demons: Collective Representations of Disease in Ceylon. *Comparative Studies in Society and History* 11:174-216.

Oesterreich, T. K.
1966 *Possession: Demoniacal and Other*. Secaucus, N.J.: Citadel Press.

Okaha, F. E.
1976 Notes on Two Shaman-Curers in Kathmandu. *Contributions to Nepalese Studies: Journal of the Institute of Nepal and Asian Studies*, Vol. 3 Special Issue (Anthropology, Health and Development):107-112.

Oldfield, H. A.
1880 *Sketches from Nepal*, Volumes 1 & 2. Delhi: Cosmo Publications.

Opler, M. E.
1936 Some Points of Comparison and Contrast Between the Treatment of Functional Disorders by Apache Shamans and Modern Psychiatric Practice. *American Journal of Psychiatry* 92:1371-1387.

Opler, M. K.
1959 Dream Analysis in Ute Indian Therapy. In *Culture and Mental Health*. M. K. Opler, ed., pp. 97-117. New York: Macmillan.

Ortner, S.

1973 On Key Symbols. *American Anthropologist* 75: 1338-1346.

Ouspensky, P. D.

1960 On the Study of Dreams and on Hypnotism. In *A New Model of the Universe*, pp. 271-307. London: Routledge & Kegan Paul Ltd.

Park, W. Z.

1938 *Shamanism in Western North America: A Study in Cultural Relationships*. Evanston: Northwestern University Press.

Paul, B.

1955 *Health, Culture and Community*. B. Paul, ed., New York: Russell Sage Foundation.

Pelto, P. J. and G. H. Pelto

1978 *Anthropological Research: The Structure of Inquiry*, Second Edition. Cambridge: Cambridge University Press.

Peters, L. G.

1978 Psychotherapy in Tamang Shamanism. *Ethos: Journal of the Society for Psychological Anthropology* 6(2):63-91.

1979 Shamanism and Medicine in Developing Nepal. *Contributions To Nepalese Studies: Journal of the Research Centre for Nepal and Asian Studies* (Kirtipur, Nepal: Tribhuvan University) VI(2): 27-43.

Peters, L. G. and D. Price-Williams

1980 Towards an Experiential Analysis of Shamanism. *American Ethnologist* 7(3):397-418.

Price, H. H.
1968 Foreword. In *Lucid Dreams* by C. E. Green. London: Hamish Hamilton.

Prince, R.
1964 Indigenous Yoruba Psychiatry. In *Magic, Faith and Healing*. A. Kiev, ed., pp. 84-120. New York: The Free Press.
1968 Can the E.E.G. Be Used in the Study of Possession States? In *Trance and Possession States*. R. Prince, ed., pp. 121-137. Montreal: R. M. Bucke Memorial Society.
1973 Mystical Experience and the Certainty of Belonging: An Alternative to Insight and Suggestion in Psychotherapy. In *Religious Systems and Psychotherapy*. R. H. Cox, ed., pp. 307-318. Springfield, Ill: Charles C. Thomas.
1976 Psychotherapy as the Manipulation of Endogenous Healing Mechanisms: A Transcultural Survey. *Transcultural Psychiatric Research Review* 13: 115-133.
1980 Religious Experience and Psychosis. *Journal of Altered States of Consciousness* 5(2):167-181.

Prince, R., A. Leighton and R. May
1968 The Therapeutic Process in Cross-Cultural Perspective: A Symposium. *American Journal of Psychiatry* 124:1171-1183.

Radcliffe-Brown, A. R.
1952 *Structure and Function in Primitive Society*. New York: The Free Press.

Radin, P.
1956 *The Trickster*. New York: Schocken Books.

Redfield, R.

1955 *The Little Community*. Chicago: University of Chicago Press.

Regmi, M. C.

1963-1968 *Land Tenure and Taxation in Nepal*, 4 Volumes. Berkeley: University of California Press.

1971 *A Study in Nepali Economic History: 1768-1846.* New Delhi: Mañjuśrī Publishing House.

1976 *Landownership in Nepal*. Berkeley: University of California Press.

Reinhard, J.

1976 Shamanism and Spirit Possession: The Definition Problem. In *Spirit Possession in the Nepal Himalayas*. J. T. Hitchcock and R. K. Jones, eds., pp. 12-23. New Delhi: Vikas Publishing House Pvt. Ltd.

Reyher, J.

1963 Free Imagery: An Uncovering Procedure. *Journal of Clinical Psychology* 19:454-459.

Ridington, R.

1969 *The Anthropology of Experience*. Paper given at Annual Meeting of the American Anthropological Association, New Orleans, Louisiana.

Riesman, P.

1977 *Freedom in Fulani Social Life*. M. Fuller, transl. Chicago: University of Chicago Press.

Rose, L. E.

1971 *Nepal: Strategy for Survival*. Delhi: Oxford University Press.

Rycroft, C.

1968 *Anxiety and Neurosis*. London: Hogarth Press.

Sargant, W.

1973 *The Mind Possessed*. New York: J. B. Lippincott.

Sasaki, Y.

1969 Psychiatric Study of the Shaman in Japan. In *Mental Health Research in Asia and the Pacific*. W. Caudill and T. Lin, eds., pp. 223-241. Honolulu: East-West Center Press.

Scheff, T.

1979 *Catharsis in Healing, Ritual and Drama*. Berkeley: University of California Press.

Seigerest, H. E.

1977 The Special Position of the Sick. In *Culture, Disease and Healing*. D. Landy, ed., pp. 388-394. New York: Macmillan Publishing Co., Inc.

Shirokogoroff, S.

1935 *Psychomental Complex of the Tungus*. London: Routledge & Kegan Paul Ltd.

Shweder, R. A.

1972 Aspects of Cognition in Zinacanteco Shamans: Experimental Results. In *Reader in Comparative Religion*. W. A. Lessa and E. Z. Vogt, eds., pp. 407-412. New York: Harper & Row.

Silverman, J.

1967 Shamans and Acute Schizophrenia. *American Anthropologist* 69:21-31.

Singer, J. L.

1971 The Vicissitudes of Imagery in Research and Clinical Use. *Contemporary Psychoanalysis* 7:163-180.

1974 *Imagery and Daydream Methods in Psychotherapy and Behavior Modification*. New York: Academic Press.

Spiro, M. E.

1965 Religious Systems and Culturally Constituted Defense Mechanisms. In *Context and Meaning in Cultural Anthropology*. M. E. Spiro, ed., pp. 100-113. New York: The Free Press.

Staal, F.

1975 *Exploring Mysticism*. Berkeley: University of California.

Stabelein, W.

1976 Mahākāla the Neo-Shaman: Master of the Ritual. In *Spirit Possession in the Nepal Himàlayas*. J. T. Hitchcock and R. L. Jones, eds., pp. 361-375. New Delhi: Vikas Publishing House Pvt. Ltd.

Stein, R. A.

1972 *Tibetan Civilization*. J. E. Stapleton Driver, transl. Stanford, California: Stanford University Press.

Sternberg, L.

1925 Divine Election in Primitive Religion. *Congrès International des Amèricanistes, Compte-Rendu de la XXIe Session*, Part 2, pp. 472-512. Göteborg.

Stiller, L. F.

1976 *The Silent Cry: The People of Nepal 1816-1839*. Kathmandu, Nepal: Sahayogi Prakashan.

Sturtevant, W. C.

1968 Categories, Percussion and Physiology. *Man* III(1):133-134.

Tart, C.

1972 State of Consciousness and State-Specific Sciences. *Science* 176:1203-1210.

1977 Putting the Pieces Together: A Conceptual Framework for Understanding Discrete States of Consciousness. In *Alternate States of Consciousness.* N. E. Zinberg, ed., pp. 158-219. New York: The Free Press.

Tibetan Book of the Dead. Lâma K. Dawa-Samdup, transl. W. Y. Evans-Wentz, ed. London: Oxford University Press (1960).

Torrey, E. F.

1972 *The Mind Game*. New York: Emerson Hall Publishers.

Tucci, G.

1961 *The Theory and Practice of the Maṇḍala, With Special Reference to the Modern Psychology of the Subconscious*. A. H. Brodrick, transl. New York: Samuel Weiser.

Turner, R. L.

1927 The People and Their Languages. In *The Gurkhas.* W. B. Northey and C. J. Morris, eds., pp. 63-73. Delhi: Cosmo Publications.

1931 *A Comparative and Etymological Dictionary of the Nepali Language*. London: Routledge and Kegan Paul Ltd.

Turner, V.

1964 An Ndembu Doctor in Practice. In *Magic, Faith and Healing*. A. Kiev, ed., pp. 230-363. New York: The Free Press.

1967a Betwixt and Between: The Liminal Period in Rites de Passage. In *The Forest of Symbols*, pp. 93-111. Ithaca: Cornell University Press.

1967b Symbols in Ndembu Ritual. In *The Forest of Symbols*, pp. 19-47. Ithaca: Cornell University Press.

1967c Introduction. In *The Forest of Symbols*, pp. 1-16. Ithaca: Cornell University Press.

1969 *The Ritual Process*. Chicago: Aldine Publishing Company.

1974 Social Dramas and Ritual Metaphors. In *Dramas, Fields, and Metaphors*, pp. 23-59. Ithaca: Cornell University Press.

1975 Chihamba the White Spirit: A Ritual Drama of the Ndembu. In *Revelation and Divination in Ndembu Ritual*, pp. 37-206. Ithaca: Cornell University Press.

Underhill, E.

1955 *Mysticism: A Study in the Nature and Development of Man's Spiritual Consciousness*. New York: Noonday Press.

UNICEF in Nepal.

1974 *Children of the Hills and Valleys* (1964-1974).

Van Den Berg, J. H.

1962 An Existential Explanation of the Guided Daydreams in Psychotherapy. *Review of Existential Psychology and Psychiatry* 2(1):5-35.

Van Eeden. F.

1969 A Study of Dreams. In *Altered States of Consciousness*. C. Tart, ed., pp. 145-158. New York: John Wiley & Sons, Inc.

Van Gennep, A.

1908 *The Rites of Passage*. M. B. Vizedom and G. L. Caffee, transl. Chicago: University of Chicago Press.

Waddell, L. A.

1894 *The Buddhism of Tibet or Lamaism*. Cambridge: W. Heffer and Sons Ltd.

Wallace, A. F. C.
1961 *Culture and Personality*. New York: Random House.
1966 *Religion: An Anthropological View*. New York: Random House.
1970 *Culture and Personality*, Second Edition. New York: Random House.

Walter, G. W.
1953 *The Living Brain*. London: Duckworth Publishing.

Wasson, R. G.
1968 Soma: Divine Mushroom of Immortality. *Ethno-Mycological Studies No. 1*. New York: Harcourt, Brace & World.

Watkins, M. M.
1976 *Waking Dreams*. New York: Harper & Row.

Watters, D.
1975 Siberian Shamanistic Traditions Among the Kham Magar of Nepal. *Contributions to Nepalese Studies: Journal of the Institute of Nepal and Asian Studies* (Kirtipur, Nepal: Tribhuvan University) 2(1):123-168.

Webb, E. J., Campbell, D. T., Schwartz, R. D. & L. Sechrest
1966 *Unobtrusive Measures: Non-reactive Research in the Social Sciences*. Chicago: Rand McNally.

West, L. J.
1967 Dissociative Reaction. In *Comprehensive Textbook of Psychiatry*. A. M. Freedman and H. Kaplan, eds., pp. 885-889. Baltimore: Williams and Wilkins Company.

Wilson, P. J.
1967 Status Ambiguity and Spirit Possession. *Man* 2(3):366-378.

Wissler, C.
1938 *The American Indian*, Third Edition. New York: Oxford University.

Woodroffe, J. (alias A. Avalon)
1974 *The Serpent Power*. New York: Dover Publications, Inc.

Yap, P. M.
1960 The Possession Syndrome: A Comparison of Hong Kong and French Findings. *Journal of Mental Science* 106:114-137.
1977 The Culture-Bound Reactive Syndromes. In *Culture, Disease and Healing*. D. Landy, ed., pp. 340-349. New York: Macmillan Publishing Co. Inc.

Zinberg, N. E.
1977 The Study of Consciousness States: Problems and Progress. In *Alternate States of Consciousness*. N. E. Zinberg, ed., pp. 1-36. New York: The Free Press.

ACKNOWLEDGEMENTS

Special thanks are extended to Professors Jacques Maquet, Douglass Price-Williams, John G. Kennedy and Walter Goldschmidt for their encouragement during all phases of research and for their reading of earlier drafts, suggestions and comments.

I wish to thank the journals and societies who have authorized me to reproduce my articles in this book:

Some parts of Chapter 1 first appeared in an article co-authored by Douglass Price-Williams entitled "Towards an Experiential Analysis of Shamanism," and are reproduced by permission of the American Ethnological Society from *American Ethnologist* 7:3, 1980:397-418.

Most of Chapter 3 is reproduced by permission of *The Journal of Transpersonal Psychology*, copyright Transpersonal Institute 1981, from an article entitled "An Experiential Study of Nepalese Shamanism," 13:1, pp. 1-26.

Most of Chapter 6 is from an article entitled "Trance, Initiation and Psychotherapy in Tamang Shamanism" and is reproduced by permission of the American Ethnological Society from *American Ethnologist* in press.

Most of Chapter 7 is from an article entitled "Psychotherapy in Tamang Shamanism" and is reproduced by permission of the Society for Psychological Anthropology from *Ethos* 6:2, 1978: 63-91.

Nirala Series

Ocean in a Drop
Yoga, Meditation and Life in the Himalayas
Swami Chandresh
ISBN 81-8250- 005-2 2006 Hard pp.348 Rs.495

Maoists in the Land of Buddha
An Analytical Study of the Maoist Insurgency in Nepal
Prakash A. Raj
ISBN 81-85693-42-0 2004 Hard pp.210 Rs.395

The Yeti
Spirit of Himalayan Forest Shamans
Larry G. Peters
ISBN 81-85693-57-9 2004 Hard pp.128 Rs.250

Rana Rule in Nepal
Shaphalya Amatya
ISBN 81-85693-67-6 2004 Hard pp.408 Rs.695

Trance, Initiation & Psychotherapy in Nepalese Shamanism
Essays on Tamang and Tibetian Shamanism
Larry G.Peters
ISBN 81-85693-79-X 2004 Hard pp.412 Rs.595

Folk Tales of Sherpa and Yeti
Collected by Shiva Dhakal
***Adapted by* Yuyutsu RD Sharma**
ISBN 81-8250-002-0 1996 Paper pp.125 Rs. 150

The Gurkha Connection
A History of Gurkha Recruitment in the British Army
Purushottam Baskota
ISBN 81-85693-77-3 2006 Paper pp.221 Rs.195

Dolpo :The Hidden Paradise
A Journey to the Endangered Sanctuary of the Himalayan Kingdom of Nepal
Karna Sakya
ISBN 81-85693-73-0 2006 Paper pp.246 Rs.250

Malla Coins of Medieval Nepal
Jagdish Chandra Regmi
ISBN 81-85693-60-9 2007 Hard Rs.295

The Dhimals: Miraculous Migrants of Himal
An Anthropological Study of a Nepalese Ethnic Group
Rishikeshab Raj Regmi
ISBN 81-8250-009-7 1991 Hard pp.269 Rs.250

The Questions of Dharma in the Mahabhatara
Birendra Mishra
ISBN 81-85693-48-X 2007 Hard pp.226 Rs.450

The Gurungs: Thunder of Himal
A Cross-Cultural Study of a Nepalese Ethnic Group
Murari P. Regmi
ISBN 81-85693-49-8 2002 Paper pp.238 Rs.295

The Gurkhas
A History of the Recruitment in the British Indian Army
Kamal Raj Singh Rathaur
ISBN 81-85693-85-4 2000 Paper pp.128 Rs.125

The Political Economy of Land, Landlessness and Migration in Nepal
Nanda R. Shrestha
ISBN 81-85693-87-0 2001 Hard pp.309 Rs.450

Tourism in Nepal
Marketing Challenges
Hari Prasad Shrestha
ISBN 81-85693-69-2 2000 Hard pp.399 Rs.495

Ethnic Conflict in Bhutan
Political and Economic Dimensions
Mathew Joseph C.
ISBN 81-85693-68-4 1999 Hard pp.251 Rs.395

Mountain Dimensions
An Altitude Geographic Analysis of Environment and Development of the Himalayas
Ram Kumar Pandey
ISBN 81-85693-43-9 1999 pp.260 Hard Rs.350

Tamang Shamans
An Ethnopsychiatric Study of Ecstasy and Healing in Nepal
Larry G. Peters
ISBN 81-8250-009-5 2007 Paper pp.179 Rs.250

Wildlife in Nepal
Rishikesh Shaha & Richard M. Mitchell
With Color Plates by **Nanda Shumsher J.B. Rana**
ISBN 81-85693-31-5 2001 Paper pp.142 Rs.250

Nepal: Missing Elements in the Development Thinking
Gunanidhi Sharma
ISBN 81-85693-66-8 2000 Hard pp.282 Rs.295

Art and Culture of Nepal
An Attempt towards Preservation
Saphalya Amatya
ISBN 81-85693-63-3 1999 Hard pp.282 Rs.295

Recent Nepal
An Analysis of Recent Democratic Upsurge and its Aftermath
Laksman Bhadur K.C.
ISBN 81-85693-24-2 1993 Hard pp.242 Rs.295

Making of Modern Nepal
A Study of History, Art and Culture of the Principalities of Western Nepal
Ram Niwas Pandey
ISBN 81-85693-37-4 1997 Hard pp.816 Rs.795

Politics and Development in Nepal:
Some Issues
Narayan Khadka
ISBN 81-85693-21-8 1994 Hard pp.477 Rs.450

Indo-Nepal Trade Relations
A Historical Analysis of Nepal's Trade with the British India
Shri Ram Upadhyaya
ISBN 81-85693-20-X 1992 pp.287 Rs.350

Secrets of Shangri-La
An Inquiry into the Lore, Legend and Culture of Nepal
Nagendra Sharma
ISBN 81-85693-18-8 1992 pp.292 Rs.250

The Taming of Tibet
A Historical Account of Compromise and Confrontation in Nepal-Tibet Relations (1900-1930)
Tirtha Prasad Mishra
ISBN 81-85693-16-1 1991 pp.324 Rs.300

Glimpses of Tourism, Airlines and Management in Nepal
B.R. Singh
ISBN 81-85693-15-3 1991 pp.128 Rs.125

Sales Promotion in Nepal
Policies and Practices
Parashar Prasad Koirala
ISBN 81-85693-14-5 1991 pp.196 Rs.225

Hindu-Buddhist Festival of Nepal
Hemant Kumar Jha
ISBN 81-85693-40-4 1996 Hard pp.117 Rs.195

Transit of Land Locked Countries and Nepal
Gajendra Mani Pradhan
ISBN 81-85693-08-0 1990 pp.240 Rs. 225

Fundamentals of Library and Information Science
A Nepalese Response
Madhusudan Sharma Subedi
ISBN 81-85693-07-4 1990 pp.229 Rs.225

Folk Culture of Nepal
An Analytical Study
Ram Dayal Rakesh
ISBN 81-85693-06-4 1990 Hard pp.129 Rs.100

A Macro-economic Study of the Nepalese Plan Performance
Gunanidhi Sharma
ISBN 81-85693-06-4 1989 pp.129

Sources of Inflation in Asia
Theory and Evidences
Raghab D. Pant
ISBN 81-85693-03-X 1988 Hard pp.118 Rs. 100

New Directions in Nepal- India Relations
Rishikesh Shaha
ISBN 81-85693-53-6 1995 Paper pp.59 Rs.65

In Nepali Language

Panaharu Khalichan : Kavitaka Dui Dashak (Poems)
Yuyustu R.D. Sharma
Hard (Forthcoming)
ISBN 81-8250-004-4 2007 Paper pp. 102 Rs. 95

Pashushala (Animal Farm) (A Novel)
Georege Orwell
Translated from the English by Bijuli Prasad Kayast
ISBN 81-8250-000-1 2004 Paper pp.96 Rs.95

Nepalko Prajatantrik Andolan Ko Itihas
Surya Mani Adhikary
ISBN 81-85693-54-4 1998 Paper pp.468 Rs. 295

Geetajanjali (Nepali)
Rabindra Nath Tagore
Translated from the Bengali by **Ramesh Bhatta & Pashupati Neopane**
ISBN 81-85693-83-8 2000 Paper pp.125

Sarpahoru Geet Sundainan
Pomes by **Shailendra Sakar**
ISBN 81-85693-97-8 1991 Hard pp.108 Rs. 60

Anyatha Ashyiaya
Pomes by Shiva Adhikari
ISBN 81-85693-51-X 2007 Paper